Stadium Stories:

St. Louis Rams

Stadium Stories™ Series

Stadium Stories:
St. Louis Rams

Rick Smith

GUILFORD, CONNECTICUT
AN IMPRINT OF THE GLOBE PEQUOT PRESS

INSIDERS' GUIDE®

Text design: Casey Shain
All photos are courtesy of Associated Press/Wide World Photos, except
where noted.
Cover photos: *front cover:* Kurt Warner; *back cover:* top, Elroy "Crazylegs"
Hirsch; bottom, George Allen with Pat Haden.

Library of Congress Cataloging-in-Publication Data
Smith, Rick, 1957-
    Stadium Stories : St. Louis Rams / Rick Smith. – 1st ed.
      p. cm. – (Stadium stories series)
    ISBN 0-7627-3793-X
    1. St. Louis Rams (Football team) I. Title. II. Series

GV956.S85S55 2005
796.332'64'0977866 – dc22   2005043410

Manufactured in the United States of America
First Edition/First Printing

To Susie, Alli, Courtney, Jeff, Conner, and Drew.
They are the wind beneath my wings.

Contents

Acknowledgments

Thank you Georgia Frontiere, John Shaw, Jay Zygmunt, Mike Martz, Bob Wallace, and Stan Kroenke, and those people who made my job not always easier, but always interesting.

Special thanks to head trainer Jim Anderson and equipment manager Todd Hewitt, two guys who have no idea how important their support and cooperation is to a PR man.

And to the players and coaches too numerous to mention, you made it fun.

Introduction

The last story in this book ends with the St. Louis Rams victory in Super Bowl XXXIV on January 30, 2000. Since then the Rams have made additional playoff appearances and lost a heart-breaking Super Bowl XXXVI game to the New England Patriots on a last-second field goal.

Under head coach Mike Martz, the Rams remained a contender despite the annual loss of top players to free agency, trades, injuries, and retirements.

Marshall Faulk, Kurt Warner, Adam Timmerman, and Torry Holt were the key player additions to the 1999 team that won the Super Bowl. Martz, who joined the coaching staff that year as offensive coordinator and who would replace the retiring Dick Vermeil after the Super Bowl, was the final ingredient. It was Martz's offense that set the NFL on its ear.

Some say that NFL stands for "Not For Long." Players, coaches, and administrators come and go. At the end of the 2004 season, there were only eight players remaining from the Rams' fifty-three-man roster that went to Atlanta for that memorable Super Bowl XXXIV.

I retired as the Rams' vice president of public relations in May of 2003, having joined the organization in February of 1992. I eagerly said yes when asked to write this book, and it was enjoyable doing the research and recalling my own experiences.

The fourth story is devoted mostly to Paul "Tank" Younger, a former Rams star with whom I worked as a member of the San Diego Chargers organization from 1977 to 1987 and with the

Rams from 1992 to 1995, when Tank retired. Tank was a friend and NFL mentor.

As work on the book progressed, the personal recollections became easier but the writing more difficult. I had joined an organization whose management and ownership had sustained withering criticism from fans and media for the direction the franchise had taken. The Rams were good to me. They made my last eleven years in the NFL a great experience.

Homer's Folly

It's not often that business moguls call upon the so-called ink-stained wretches of the media for assistance. But that's what the founders of the Cleveland franchise of the American Football League did in 1936. The new professional circuit was being formed, one of many that would challenge the National Football League over the years. Cleveland was one of the selected cities. Owner Homer Marshman and general manager Damon "Buzz" Wetzel, leaders of the group financing the effort, sought the advice of sportswriters from the *Cleveland Plain Dealer* and the *Cleveland Press*. "We need a name," said Wetzel. "What do you think?"

"Keep it short, so it will fit into a headline," said one of the newspapermen. That was music to Marshman's and Wetzel's ears. Maybe it was coincidence.

"Fordham was a big football school at the time," remembered Marshman in an interview years later with Hal Lebovitz of the *Plain Dealer*. "This was during the era of Vince Lombardi and the Seven Blocks of Granite." The Catholic university in the Bronx borough went by the nickname "Rams."

Fordham was the favorite team of Wetzel, who was a former Ohio State player, and Marshman liked the sound of Rams. So the AFL franchise became known as the Cleveland Rams. Now, almost seventy years later, Rams remains one of the great names in team sports: one syllable, a perfect fit in any medium, and masculine. You'll never see or hear the name shortened, as so many other team names are in print, electronic media, and conversation.

One could go back more than a hundred years and find another example of the Ohio community's use of word economy. General Moses Cleaveland founded the City of Cleaveland in 1796. However, Cleaveland was changed to its present spelling in 1831 in order to fit the city's name on a newspaper masthead.

With more than 800,000 residents in the 1930s, Cleveland was the fifth largest city in the United States, but it was not impressed with pro football. The Cleveland Panthers were part of an earlier incarnation of the AFL in 1926. That league went under after one season. There also were the Cleveland Tigers in the NFL's inaugural 1920 season, the Cleveland Indians of the NFL in 1921 and 1923, and the Cleveland Bulldogs of the NFL in 1925 and 1927.

Major League Baseball was firmly entrenched, having been played in Cleveland as early as 1879, and the Cleveland Indians won the World Series in 1920. Cleveland Stadium, hard by Lake Erie with a sprawling 74,000 seats, was one of the largest in the country. James Cleveland "Jesse" Owens of nearby East Technical High and Ohio State University was a national hero in 1936 after exploding Hitler's Aryan myth by winning four gold medals in the Berlin Olympics. That same year an eighteen-year-old flame-throwing pitcher named Bob Feller came out of the Iowa cornfields and embarked on a brilliant career with baseball's Indians.

There had been other, lesser known but no less impressive footnotes in the city's history. LifeSavers candy was first tasted in Cleveland in 1891. The comic book character Superman emerged from the creative minds of a pair of Cleveland artists in 1933. And well-known gangster nemesis Elliott Ness became the city's safety director in 1935.

The AFL Rams, while successful on the field with a 5–2–2 record in their inaugural season, did not capture Cleveland's fancy. Attendance was not just sparse, it was virtually nonexistent. Homer Marshman was in no mood to continue. Dan Hanna, one of the owner's investors and the publisher of a Cleveland newspaper, was more upbeat when he lunched with Marshman at the downtown Union Club after the season.

Mistake by the Lake

During their tenure in Cleveland, the Rams played home games at Cleveland Stadium (also known as Municipal Stadium), League Park, and Shaw Stadium. Cleveland Stadium, the largest of the facilities, hosted the Rams' 28–0 loss to Detroit in the first regular season game in franchise history in 1937.

The stadium also was derisively called the "Mistake by the Lake," because original plans for the park were drawn in hopes that Cleveland could attract the 1932 Summer Olympic Games. Instead, by the time Cleveland Stadium officially opened in the summer of 1931, the games had been awarded to Los Angeles.

Cleveland Stadium in 1995.

As Marshman recounted to Lebovitz, he said to Hanna, "Count me out. This American League is a failure." Hanna was undeterred. "What do you think about the NFL?" he asked. "Do you think we could get in?" Hanna either was not concerned or did not know about Cleveland's earlier, failed attempts in the established league.

Marshman agreed to call NFL commissioner Joe Carr and test the NFL's attitude toward expansion and Cleveland. Carr, who had helped keep the struggling NFL afloat since 1921, was receptive. He encouraged Marshman to attend the NFL meeting in Chicago in February of 1937.

The Cleveland executive felt good vibes going in. The news media said Cleveland was the favorite to become the NFL's tenth team. After making his presentation, Marshman was asked to take a seat. Representatives from Houston, Los Angeles, and other cities then made pitches, received polite thank-yous, and were ushered out.

At this point George Preston Marshall, the owner of the Washington Redskins, stood up and said, "I move we give the franchise to Cleveland." As Marshman recalled later, "It was a setup. They had decided on us in advance. They wanted ten teams, all in the Midwest or East." Travel and other expenses obviously played a major part in the NFL's decision.

Marshman prepared to leave and telephone Hanna when he was stopped. "They asked me, 'Are you prepared to pay for the franchise—now?'" Homer's new partners wanted him to come up with a $10,000 membership fee immediately. Marshman didn't have the money, but he pulled out his billfold and wrote a check, signing his name with a flourish.

Homer had just $7,000 in his bank account, but the Chicago meeting was on a Friday, so Marshman hurried back to Cleveland, got $5,000 from Hanna, rushed to the bank on Monday, and deposited the $5,000 to cover the check. "This was the Depression, you know," said Marshman, who not only had lost money with the football team but whose law practice also had suffered.

Cleveland thus began preparations for its fifth attempt at pro football. They still were known as the Rams, and there were a few holdover players from the 1936 AFL team, plus ten rookies from the NFL's college draft in 1937. (The draft had been instituted just one year earlier.) The NFL also had made a first selection for "the new team" before the franchise had been awarded. That player was fullback Johnny Drake of Purdue.

Next on the agenda was the appointment of a coach. The Rams had decided to further honor Fordham University by wearing uniforms of the red and black colors of the collegians. They also went for a coach with a collegiate background, but the similarity ended there.

In fifty-four-year-old Hugo Bezdek, who had not coached in eight years, the Rams selected the first foreign-born NFL head coach and the only man ever to serve as an NFL head coach and a Major League Baseball manager.

Bezdek may have lost a few miles per hour on his figurative fastball, but he had an outstanding football background and was recommended by Bert Bell, the respected owner of the Philadelphia Eagles, who also was a member of the NFL's finance committee and a future league commissioner.

Born in Czechoslovakia and raised from age five in Chicago, Bezdek played fullback under Amos Alonzo Stagg at the University of Chicago. After graduating in 1906, Bezdek immediately was named head coach at the University of Oregon, where he went undefeated in his first season. That was followed by a winning record in five seasons as head coach at Arkansas, including 7–0 in 1909.

Bezdek returned to Oregon in 1913 and coached at that school for six more seasons. His team was 6–0–1 and beat Pennsylvania in the 1917 Rose Bowl. Hugo also somehow found time to work as a West Coast scout for baseball's Pittsburgh Pirates. In the middle of the 1917 season, the last-place Pirates made him their manager.

Bezdek rallied the Pirates to fourth-place finishes in 1918 and 1919. While still managing the Pirates in 1918, he also was named the head coach and athletic director at Penn State. Through 1929 Bezdek's coaching record at Penn State was 65–30–11. Included was a twenty-nine-game unbeaten streak and an appearance in the 1923 Rose Bowl against the University of Southern California. Bezdek's collegiate coaching record was an impressive 124–54–16. His baseball managing record was 166–187.

In 1929 Bezdek retired from coaching. He had been known as a coach whose players looked forward to games because they were much easier than his practices. He also was credited with pioneering the use of a passing attack from spread formations and for inventing the Single Wing "spinner" play, in which the fullback spins 180 degrees before advancing the ball by pass or run.

Hugo enjoyed a more leisurely life as the athletic director at Penn State until the call came from the Rams. He may not have taken the job had he known better.

The Rams' first game in 1937—they had no preseason games, they teed it up in league play—was witnessed by an estimated 15,000 fans in Cleveland Stadium. The Detroit Lions won 28–0, scoring one touchdown on a blocked forward pass that was returned 45 yards and another on a bad snap from center that rolled into the Rams end zone and was covered by a Detroit player.

After defeating Philadelphia 21–3 in their second game, the Rams flattened out with nine consecutive losses, never scoring more than 10 points in any game. The ignominious finish to the season came in the last home game. A Cleveland charitable organization was given the license to promote the contest. A crowd generously estimated at 5,000 gathered amid freezing, snowbound weather and watched rookie quarterback Sammy Baugh lead the Washington Redskins to a 16–7 victory. "Actually, almost nobody showed up except the players," said Marshman.

Following their debut in Cleveland Stadium, the Rams moved their remaining home games to League Park, which was built in 1891. The Rams didn't return to Cleveland Stadium in 1938 because of its cavernous expanse—and because they couldn't afford the rent. The Rams then moved to Shaw Stadium, which was a high school facility.

Bezdek's 1938 squad staggered out of the gate to an 0–3 start. An NFL coach on a short leash seldom survives such a poor start after a losing year. Sure enough, Bezdek got what is known in the profession as the "Big Haircut." He was fired and

Home, Sweet Homes

Here are the stadiums in which the Rams have played their home games since the inception of the franchise:

NAME	CITY	YEARS
League Park	Cleveland	1937, 1942, 1944–45
Cleveland Stadium	Cleveland	1937, 1939–41, 1945
Shaw Stadium	Cleveland	1938
Memorial Coliseum	Los Angeles	1946–79
Anaheim Stadium	Anaheim	1980–94
Busch Stadium	St. Louis	1995
Trans World Dome	St. Louis	1995–present

replaced by Art "Pappy" Lewis, a starting offensive lineman who years later had a successful run at West Virginia University. Bezdek was not the only casualty. General manager Buzz Wetzel was also cashiered.

Lewis was not destined for a long tenure. He had been Bezdek's assistant, but Lewis's new title was "temporary head coach." Despite this thin portfolio, the Rams were 4–4 under Lewis. They drew their largest crowd in two seasons when the powerful Green Bay Packers attracted more than 18,000 fans to a game in late October. Coming off three straight victories, the Rams crashed back to earth, losing 28–7.

Marshman conceded that Lewis was effective as "temporary head coach," but attendance was poor. A brand-name coach was needed.

So the Rams turned to Earl "Dutch" Clark, a legendary Detroit Lions quarterback whose powerful profile on the cover of *Life* magazine in 1937 remains one of the great sports photographs of all time.

Clark, who eventually was a charter inductee in the Pro Football Hall of Fame in 1963, had been an all-pro player in six of his seven seasons. He was one of the NFL's last dropkick specialists. Clark also ran the ball well and one year completed 54 percent of his passes when the NFL average was only 36 percent.

As the quarterback in the Single Wing, Clark called the plays. In 1936 Clark helped the Lions set a club rushing record that lasted until 1972. Clark also led the league in scoring three times. He kicked field goals and extra points and overcame a major hurdle throughout his career: Clark's eyesight was so poor that he had trouble locating his receivers.

Along with Clark's arrival in Cleveland, the Rams personnel improved. Rookie tailback Parker Hall won the Joe Carr Trophy as the NFL's most valuable player for 1939. End Jim Benton, who would set an NFL record with 303 yards receiving in a game in 1945, also helped bolster the offense.

The team moved its home games back into Cleveland Stadium in 1939 and finished 5–5–1, its first nonlosing record. The NFL seemed to be catching on in the city. There were crowds of 28,000 and 30,000 for late-season games. Marshman and his partners, which now numbered more than twenty, were so pleased with Clark that he was elected to the franchise's board of directors and named vice president. Attendance dwindled again, though, as the Rams slipped to 4–6–1 in 1940.

There was more than an approaching war as the months rolled on in 1941. Before his death Homer Marshman looked back on his five years in pro football. "We had been paying 'Irish dividends' each year," he told Hal Lebovitz. "That was an expression meaning we had lost money . . . a few thousand every year. We had to keep adding partners at $1,000 each every so often, just to keep afloat." Pretty soon, however, Homer's pro football venture would turn a profit.

Reeves, War, and a Championship

Homer Marshman and his twenty-three associates fought the good fight for four years, but they did not have much to show for their efforts. So Marshman listened when he received a telephone call from Daniel F. Reeves not long after the 1940 season. Reeves, a twenty-nine-year-old New Yorker who owned a chain of grocery stores with his father, wanted to buy the Rams. He submitted an offer of $100,000. After some negotiation, Reeves came up to $135,000. "When Dan said that, I convened a meeting, and just about everyone in our group said, 'Grab it!'" said Marshman. "It meant a small profit for all of us."

In June of 1941 Reeves and his partner, Frederick Levy Jr., officially assumed control of the team, with Reeves running the day-to-day operation. A former Georgetown University athlete, Reeves had previously been unsuccessful in attempts to buy the Pittsburgh Steelers and the Philadelphia Eagles.

Reeves's NFL partners had no idea what kind of man was now in their midst. The nine other NFL owners had scraped for years to keep their franchises alive during tough times in the older, industrial cities of the Midwest and East. It was not easy to be a forward thinker when survival was all that mattered. Reeves, young and urbane, had a vision for pro football. Over the next thirty years, his name would be synonymous with many of the innovations and policies that elevated the NFL into America's most popular game.

The NFL was far from such stature in the summer of 1941. Three great moments in baseball dominated the sports land-scape: Joe DiMaggio's fifty-six-game hitting streak; Ted Williams's dramatic ninth-inning home run to win the All-Star game for the American League; and Williams's .406 season batting average.

Meanwhile the 1941 NFL season began in doubt and ended in war. The Rams opened the season against the Pittsburgh Steelers in the Rubber Bowl stadium in Akron, about 30 miles from Cleveland. Levy, attending with Reeves, was gaga ("Is it this easy?") after the Rams' Dante Magnani returned the opening kickoff 95 yards for a touchdown. The crowd of 23,783, their largest in two seasons, saw the Rams win, 17–14. They followed that victory with a 10–6 win over the Cardinals in Chicago.

The promising start was met with a string of losses in the next nine games. The season mercifully ended on November 23, fourteen days before the Japanese attacked American military installations at Pearl Harbor in Hawaii.

The Rams and the NFL moved forward uncertainly in 1942. Reeves became a lieutenant in the army. Many players were called to service. Some worked in war plants while they played football. Still coached by Dutch Clark, the Rams finished with a 5–6 record. They were outscored 181–62 while losing four of their last five games. A crowd of 4,023 witnessed the last home game of the season against Detroit.

Against this backdrop Reeves sought permission to suspend operation in 1943. The NFL agreed and continued without Cleveland. The Rams rejoined the league in 1944, with Reeves choosing Charles "Chili" Walsh as general manager. Walsh played for Knute Rockne at Notre Dame in the 1920s and had been around pro football.

"Chili" then hired "Buff" as head coach. Aldo Donelli was known as Buff because of his affinity for showman Buffalo Bill Cody. Donelli's circuitous route to the Rams was not unlike that of a Cody road show, reflective of the NFL's shaky footing and cash-and-carry approach to business at that time.

When he passed away at age eighty-seven in 1994, Donelli was remembered as the coach who led Columbia University to its only Ivy League championship in 1963. His obituary in the *New York Times* noted that Donelli had "nailed down two singular footnotes to sports history: one as the only American to score a goal in the 1934 World Cup and the other as the only man to coach a college and National Football League team at the same time."

An outstanding soccer player, who scored the only United States goal in the 1934 World Cup in a 7–1 loss to Italy, Donelli was retired by 1941 and had returned to his hometown as football coach at Duquesne University in Pittsburgh.

Duquesne's Dukes were headed to an undefeated season, but the situation was different for the Pittsburgh pro team. Since joining the NFL in 1933, owner Art Rooney's team, known as the Pirates, had posted an overall record of 25–62–5. After the 1940 season Rooney sold the franchise to Alexis Thompson, then bought part interest in the Philadelphia Eagles from owner Bert Bell.

Rooney and Bell traded the Eagles to Thompson for the Pirates a few months later and renamed their franchise the Pittsburgh Steelers. The change in names did not mean a change in fortune. Bell coached the first two games of the 1941 season, including the loss to the Rams, and stepped down.

Desperate, Rooney turned to Donelli. An agreement was reached that Buff would coach the Steelers in the morning and coach the Dukes in the afternoon. After five games—all losses—Donelli received an ultimatum from NFL commissioner Elmer Layden: Choose one job or the other. "The Buffer" chose Duquesne.

When Duquesne suspended football in 1943, Donelli hooked on as an assistant coach with the NFL's Brooklyn Dodgers football team. He then came out of soccer retirement and played for the Morgan Strasser team of Pittsburgh in the 1944 U.S. Open Cup final against Brooklyn Hispano in the New York Polo Grounds. He joined the Rams as head coach a few days later.

Finding a coach was easier than finding players. Some of the Rams had been loaned to other clubs in 1943. Others had gone into the military or retired. Walsh offered a $100 finder's fee to anyone recommending a player who made the club. A pickup squad of Rams finished the 1944 season with a 4–6 record. More significant were rumors that Cleveland taxicab honcho Arthur McBride was going to head a Cleveland franchise in a new professional league that would challenge the NFL. McBride would name Paul Brown as head coach. Brown had established a legendary record at Massillon High, Ohio State, and with the Great Lakes service team. Donelli left after the 1944 season and entered the navy. Walsh named as coach his brother Adam, who also had played for Rockne at Notre Dame.

The war was coming to an end in the early days of 1945. There was a spirit of revival in Cleveland, but the Rams did not appear revived, even though they had some good players: Jim Benton, Fred Gehrke, Jim Gillette, Milan Lazetich, Steve Pritko, Mike Scarry, Gil Bouley, Red Hickey, and Riley "Rattlesnake" Matheson, who had twice been bitten by rattlesnakes and survived. It was said that the snakes died.

Another name for the roster was Bob Waterfield, a quarterback from UCLA. Waterfield had led UCLA to a 1943 Rose Bowl victory over Georgia but hadn't been selected by Cleveland until the third round of the 1944 NFL draft. Forty-one other players were picked before the handsome, curly-haired, triple-threat player from Los Angeles's San Fernando Valley.

Waterfield also was married to his former Van Nuys High School sweetheart, actress Jane Russell. She had recently starred in Howard Hughes's *The Outlaw*, a movie about cowboy bad guy

Bob Waterfield and Jane
Russell brought glamour to
football and Hollywood.

Billy the Kid that was best known for the steamy and controversial love scenes involving Russell and costar Jack Buetel.

Despite Waterfield's quick and positive grasp of the offense and a 3–1 preseason record, the Rams were not resonating in Cleveland. Attendance was fewer than 11,000 for the opener, a 21–0 victory over the Chicago Cardinals. They drew almost 20,000 for a 17–0 victory over the Chicago Bears, and someone took notice.

"I received a telephone call from *Life* magazine the day after we beat the Bears," remembered Nate Wallack, who spent a career in public relations for baseball's Cleveland Indians and football's Cleveland Rams and Browns.

Life wanted to do a cover story on Waterfield and Russell. "But the studio did not want to publicize the fact that she was married," said Wallack, who visited Jane at the couple's suite in the St. Regis Hotel. Wallack recalled when he told Russell of the problem with the studio. "I'll never forget what she said: 'I'll cooperate with you on anything that is good for Robert and the Rams.'"

The Sporting News went so far as to describe Mrs. Waterfield as "friendly, gracious, without any of the airs of a movie queen." Not stopping there, the publication added that Jane did "her own housekeeping, marketing, and cooking."

The Rams improved their record to 4–0 with a 27–14 victory over Green Bay, the 1944 NFL champion, and a 41–21 win over the Chicago Bears. In the middle of a four-game road trip, they were beaten in week five in Philadelphia but recovered to defeat the New York Giants before more than 46,000 fans at the Polo Grounds. It was the largest crowd ever to see the Cleveland Rams.

With a 5–1 record, the Rams returned home for a mid-November game against the Packers, their chief rivals in the Western Division. Ticket demand stretched League Park to its limit, but Chili Walsh rejected a suggestion that the game be moved to Cleveland Stadium. Walsh instead had portable bleachers constructed along League Park's outfield wall. A small press box went up behind the bleachers. "I was standing in the press box when the game started," said Wallack. "All of a sudden it looked as though the whole ball park was moving."

The temporary bleachers collapsed. One person sustained a broken leg. Miraculously, there were no other serious injuries, and fans observed the rest of the game from the outfield sideline. A crowd of 28,686 watched the Rams run their record to 6–1 with a 20–7 victory.

Two weeks after the victory over the Packers, the Rams faced a final hurdle as they closed in on a Western Division championship. They met the Lions in Detroit's traditional Thanksgiving Day game at Briggs Stadium. The Rams defeated the Lions 28–21. End Jim Benton caught 10 passes for 303 yards, a yardage record that would stand in the NFL for forty years.

Waterfield's mastery of the T-formation and the bootleg play had helped turn the Rams into the NFL's most dangerous offense. They averaged 355 yards a game. Running backs Jim Gillette and Fred Gehrke averaged better than 6 yards rushing, and Benton, a tall receiver from Arkansas, blossomed into one of the NFL's top long-range receiving threats. Benton caught 45 passes for a 23.7-yard average, and he scored 8 touchdowns.

The Rams' 8–1 record carried them into the NFL Championship Game against Washington. The game matched two future Pro Football Hall of Fame quarterbacks, Waterfield and the Redskins' Sammy Baugh. The memorable NFL title game is not only known for the Rams' 15–14 victory, but also for the role played by the Cleveland Stadium goal post crossbars and for the

The Rams celebrate their Western Division Championship Game victory over the Detroit Lions in 1945.

contributions of two nonplayers: Bill John, a slight man with horned-rim glasses who was the Rams business manager; and Emil Bossard, a legendary NFL groundskeeper.

There were two weeks between the final regular season game and the championship game. John, who was concerned about a frozen field occurring in typical mid-December Cleveland, had taken out newspaper advertisements in Sandusky 61 miles west all the way to Youngstown 75 miles east for hay. He negotiated the delivery of almost 9,000 bales, a stunning accomplishment, considering not many cold Ohio farmers could afford to part with winter straw and hay intended for their livestock. The hay was spread over the playing field, and a tarp was laid on top of the hay. The Rams waited. Game week began with mild weather. Ticket sales were brisk—almost 40,000 sold by four days before the game.

Goodbye, mild weather. When John arose at 3:30 A.M. on game day, he saw a blanket of snow on his front lawn. He drove to the lakefront stadium. It was eight degrees below zero, and a

The 300-Yard Club

Rams receivers have produced two of the three most prolific pass-catching days in NFL history. The league marks for most receiving in a game:

336 Willie "Flipper" Anderson
     Los Angeles Rams vs. New Orleans Saints
     November 26, 1989 (overtime)

309 Stephone Paige
     Kansas City Chiefs vs. San Diego Chargers
     December 22, 1985

303 Jim Benton
     Cleveland Rams vs. Detroit Lions
     November 22, 1945

The Washington Redskins field-goal attempt in the final minutes of the 1945 NFL Championship Game came up short, and the Rams emerged victorious.

cutting wind blew from the north. John and Bossard had hired more than 300 men for the job of clearing and preparing the field and sweeping the stands. Some were servicemen back from the war. Others were hoboes or drifters waiting to catch the next Baltimore & Ohio boxcar out of town.

At 7:30 A.M., Bossard stood under the west goal posts and began deploying his help. Four and a half hours later, the field had been cleared. John notified Reeves, who had given John the necessary resources: "As much as you need to make the field first class." Kickoff was less than an hour away. The temperature had risen to six degrees, but disaster loomed. As soon as the insulation was removed, the field froze. John and Bossard shook their heads: a noble effort gone unrewarded.

The footing was treacherous, but the Redskins, remembering that the New York Giants had worn tennis shoes on an icy field against the Bears in the 1934 NFL Championship Game, came prepared with rubber-soled shoes. The Rams had none. Adam Walsh pleaded with Washington coach Dud DeGroot not to put the Redskins in their sneakers.

"I'd appreciate it if we could play this game on even terms," said Walsh. In a gesture of sportsmanship, DeGroot agreed.

While players skidded on the field, a pipe broke in the upper deck, cascading water that immediately turned into a frozen waterfall. Many in the announced crowd of 32,178 burned hay to keep warm.

Baugh went back to pass in his own end zone in the first quarter. Floyd Konetsky, rushing in, tipped the ball, which hit the crossbar and bounced back into the end zone for a safety and two points for the Rams.

The two points would be pivotal. Frank Filchock, replacing Baugh who had sore ribs, passed to Steve Bagarus to put the Redskins ahead in the second quarter. Waterfield responded with a touchdown pass to Benton. At this point the goal posts came into play again. Waterfield's point-after-touchdown kick was partially blocked and hit the crossbar, but it fell over for a 9–7

Rule Change

The Rams were awarded a critical safety in the 1945 NFL title game when Washington quarterback Sammy Baugh attempted a pass from his own end zone that hit the goal post and bounced away. Because of that play, the NFL changed a rule. Beginning in 1946 any pass thrown from behind the line that hit either team's goal post or crossbar was considered incomplete and ruled a dead ball.

At the time, of course, the goal posts were located on each team's goal line. It was not until 1974 that the league moved the goal posts to the back of the end zone, where they are today.

lead. Waterfield threw one more touchdown pass in the second half, and the Rams held on for a 15–14 victory.

Despite the weather the game set several financial records, including gross receipts of $164,542.40. The winning Rams each earned $1,469.74. The victory was the climax to a long, hard struggle in the determined Ohio city, but Rams owner Dan Reeves already had made up his mind that his team's future was not in Cleveland.

The Land of Milk and Honey

Dan Reeves saw opportunity and untapped promise when he looked west. Most NFL owners in the 1940s saw only as far as their noses. Reeves had claimed losses of up to $50,000 despite winning the NFL championship in 1945. He wanted to move the Cleveland Rams to Los Angeles, almost 2,000 miles from the nearest NFL franchises in Chicago. Why Los Angeles? Because no major league franchise in any sport had ever located on the Pacific Coast.

There were some drawbacks, however. For instance, commercial air travel still was in its infant stages. The distance from New York to Los Angeles took almost twice as long as the same trip today. In addition there was tradition only for college football in Los Angeles, where the University of Southern California and the Rose Bowl game held sway. The 100,000-seat Los Angeles Memorial Coliseum, built for the 1932 Olympics, was a monument to amateur sport. And there was the looming prospect of yet another pro football war, with the advent of the All-America Football Conference in 1946. The AAFC was placing a team in Los Angeles, but that problem also would exist in Cleveland.

Reeves's NFL partners considered all of these factors, but they had only one real concern: money. The owners were old-line entrepreneurs, football lifers who had struggled to stay in business during the NFL's first hesitant steps in the 1920s, through the Depression in the 1930s, and amidst a world war in the first half of the 1940s. Television and its potential source of income still was a few years away. The owners didn't like the idea of stretching thin budgets with greatly increased travel expense and inherent logistical problems.

But pro football in this massive corner of Southern California had existed in some form since George Halas and the Chicago Bears barnstormed there with postseason exhibitions beginning in the 1920s. There had also been the one-year venture of the Los Angeles Buccaneers in the National Football League in 1926, but the Buccaneers did not even play in Los Angeles. The Buccaneers were actually based in Chicago, and they played all of their games on the road.

There was another franchise from Los Angeles in 1926, but it was in the American Football League, and the team played a road-only schedule. The AFL team originally was called the Wilson Club, with a Washington designation. Eventually the team became known as the Los Angeles Wildcats, named after its star player, Wildcat Wilson. Almost all of the Wildcats players were products of West Coast universities, particularly Stanford, Gonzaga, and Washington.

Then there was the Los Angeles Bulldogs, who won championships in 1937 and 1939 in two later, different AFLs and who compiled a 5–4–3 record in games against NFL teams. And the Pacific Coast Professional Football League, which operated from 1940 to 1947, boasted two successful Los Angeles franchises: the Hollywood Bears, who played their home games at Gilmore Stadium; and the Bulldogs, who played at Wrigley Field in south central Los Angeles.

Redskins owner George Preston Marshall, *Los Angeles Times* sports editor Bill Henry, and promoter Tom Gallery additionally established a postseason Pro Bowl game in Los Angeles at this time. The NFL champion played a team of pro all-stars following the 1938, 1939, and 1940 seasons.

Reeves, thirty-three years old and full of energy and determination, was confident he could be successful in this huge market that offered not only great weather but also the potential for unrelenting growth. He carried the fight to his NFL partners after his request to move was denied in a 6–4 vote. "And you call this a *national* league?" he shouted, momentarily storming out of a meeting room and threatening to pull his franchise from the NFL. Reeves even suggested a possible move to Dallas, but that was rejected, also.

Star running back Kenny Washington (center) in a movie rehearsal with Sonny Tufts (left) and Victor Mature (right).

The Rams future was not the only item on the league meeting agenda in early January of 1946. Elmer Layden's contract as commissioner was not renewed, and he was succeeded by Bert Bell. Free substitution during games was withdrawn, and substitutions were limited to no more than three players at one time. Forward passes were automatically incomplete upon striking goal posts. Reeves was an interested party to all of these issues, but he spent most of the time lobbying his NFL partners and working the room. He finally won over the other owners by agreeing to pay each visiting NFL team $5,000 above the visitors' net gate receipts to cover travel costs.

Approval meant the Rams avoided a thorny situation in Cleveland. Arthur McBride's All-America Football Conference franchise had negotiated a long-term lease for use of Cleveland Stadium, and McBride hired Paul Brown, the most successful high school (Massillon, Ohio), college (Ohio State), and military (Great Lakes Navy) coach in the game.

There were hurdles to clear in California, however. The key to moving west was securing permission to play in the Los Angeles Coliseum. The rival AAFC's Los Angeles Dons were also trying to lease the stadium.

The Dons challenged the Coliseum not to let in the NFL team. "The AAFC people said we shouldn't be dealing with the NFL, that the NFL had an unwritten rule of no colored [players]," said Bill Nicholas, a member of the Coliseum Commission from its inception in September of 1945. The Coliseum Commission apparently agreed; it insisted that, before issuing a lease to the Rams, a tryout be awarded to local African-American player Kenny Washington.

Reeves's altruism was later questioned in regard to his signing of black players one year before Jackie Robinson broke the color line in baseball and thirteen years after the NFL had enacted an unofficial hands-off policy. Perhaps Reeves did not act in the same spirit as the Brooklyn Dodgers' Branch Rickey, who signed Robinson, but Reeves once again went against the grain.

L.A. Story

The NFL was the first of the major professional sports leagues to expand to the West Coast. Ironically, though, the league has not had a team in Los Angeles, the nation's second largest market, since the Rams left after the 1994 season. Here are the pro football franchises that have represented Los Angeles over the years:

Team	League	Years
Los Angeles Buccaneers	National Football League	1926
Los Angeles Wildcats	American Football League	1926
Los Angeles Bulldogs	American Football League	1937
Los Angeles Bulldogs	American Professional Football League	1939
Los Angeles Rams	National Football League	1946–94
Los Angeles Dons	All-America Football Conference	1946–49
Southern California Sun	World Football League	1974–76
Los Angeles Raiders	National Football League	1982–94
Los Angeles Express	United States Football League	1983–85
Los Angeles Xtreme	XFL	2001–05

Rams backfield coach Bob Snyder remembered: "All hell broke loose [among NFL owners] when word got around [that Washington might be signed]. There was quite a bit of objection, but Reeves did it. He deserved the credit." When Washington came to terms on March 21, 1946, he became the first African-American to sign with a major professional league team in the modern era. No black player had been active in the NFL since 1933.

Washington was a product of East Los Angeles's Lincoln High and was a teammate of Jackie Robinson's at UCLA. As the star of the Hollywood Bears, Washington also was the most significant player in the Pacific Coast Professional Football League. He set school records in rushing and passing at UCLA, led the nation in rushing in 1939, and played against the Green Bay Packers in the 1940 Chicago College All-Star Game. He was introduced to the owner and coach of the Chicago Bears after the game.

"I remember George Halas asking me to stay around Chicago to see what he could do," said Washington, who died of a rare circulatory disease at age fifty-two in 1971. "I waited about a week, and then I was told he couldn't use me." Washington went back home and played the next six seasons in the PCPFL. He was twenty-nine when he signed with the Rams and had two aching knees. Not the player he had been, Washington still led the Rams in rushing in 1947 and averaged 6.1 yards a carry in his three seasons with the club.

Another local black athlete was signed by the Rams on May 7, 1946. Woody Strode had been a football and decathlon standout at UCLA and had played for the Los Angeles semipro teams and in the military during World War II. Strode was almost thirty-two when he came to the Rams. He played sparingly before

Los Angeles Coliseum, for many years the home field of the Rams.

retiring to a long career in Hollywood, where he was cast in a dozen Westerns directed by John Ford, including several starring John Wayne. Strode appeared in more than seventy films in all and was a fixture on the Southern California professional wrestling circuit when matches were televised virtually every night of the week in the early 1950s.

Reeves, meanwhile, was wrestling with the Coliseum Commission and was able to strike a deal after agreeing to play one exhibition game each year with proceeds going to charity. The *Los Angeles Times* Charity Game, as it became known, was an instant success. With the Washington Redskins meeting the Rams in a rematch of the 1945 NFL Championship Game, a crowd of more than 95,000 showed up to see the Rams win 16–14. The annual *Times* Charity Game had an average attendance of more than 80,000 per game into the 1970s.

The Rams did not achieve exclusive use of the Coliseum, however, sharing the facility on alternate Sundays with the AAFC's Dons. Fighting with the Dons for the pro football fan allegiance became a bitter struggle. The addition of Washington and Strode provided a nice publicity bounce for the new team, but Reeves gained additional cachet when he signed halfback Tom Harmon, the 1940 Heisman Trophy winner from the University of Michigan, and quarterback Jim Hardy, who had led USC to the Rose Bowl.

Still the Rams were not an overnight success. Attendance fluctuated wildly in the early years. The Philadelphia Eagles attracted only 30,500 for the Los Angeles Rams' first league game in 1946, but the Chicago Bears pulled 68,831 later in the season. Attendance for a 1947 game with the powerful Chicago Cardinals brought out almost 70,000 fans, but three weeks later there weren't 20,000 on hand for a game with the Boston Yankees. The Rams drew fewer than 13,000 fans for the home opener with the Detroit Lions in 1948 but more than 56,000 for the Bears.

In addition to the rival Dons, the Rams also felt the presence of Coliseum tenants USC and UCLA. NFL teams today have huge season-ticket sales banked before the first towel is issued in training camp. The Rams, despite some outstanding teams, usually sold no more than 35,000 season seats in the cavernous Coliseum. The incentive for season tickets did not exist. There always were available tickets if someone decided at the last minute on Sunday to go to a game.

If Reeves was discouraged, it did not show. He instituted a "Free Football for Kids" program that enabled youngsters to enjoy the game in their formative years and hopefully become full-time fans as adults. His experimentation in the early years of television provided the groundwork for the NFL's policy for decades. Reeves televised road games and home games, unless attendance fell below a predetermined level.

Reeves became the first pro football owner to employ a full-time scouting staff for evaluation of college players, and he adopted halfback Fred Gehrke's novel idea to paint an insignia on the team's helmets. Gehrke was an industrial illustrator at a Los Angeles aviation company during the off-season. He had studied art at Colorado State, and he didn't like the look of the Rams' plain, brown leather headgear. In 1947 Fred painted a picture of what he thought the Rams helmet should look like.

Gehrke took the painting to head coach Bob Snyder. "He couldn't tell much from that, so he gave me a helmet to take home and told me to paint it the way I liked," Gehrke remembered. Gehrke stayed up all night. "I drew the ram horns on with chalk and painted the rest of the helmet in blue. Then I came back inside the chalk lines with the gold for the horns. It wasn't easy. The leather was not even."

Lasting Legacy

In 2000 when the St. Louis Rams contemplated a new
uniform design and new colors, I fielded a phone
inquiry from the retired general manager of the Denver
Broncos. "She's not going to change the helmet, is
she?" Fred Gehrke asked plaintively. Rams owner
Georgia Frontiere later assured Gehrke that the helmet
design was "never" going to be altered or discarded.
Fred passed away at age eighty-two in 2002, comfort-
able with his legacy and with his marvelous contribution to the Rams and to football on all levels.

Fred was anxious that Snyder would not be impressed. The
coach instead showed the painted helmet to the other coaches
and staff. Dan Reeves liked the rendition and commissioned
Gehrke to paint all of the team's helmets in the off-season for one
dollar each.

When the Rams took the field in 1948, it was with their
newly decorated headgear. But Gehrke's work was not done. The
concussive nature of the game, with players going helmet to
helmet, resulted in the paint constantly chipping. Gehrke took
the helmets home after each game and repainted them. He
would have to paint the helmets only one year, however. In 1949,
helmet manufacturer Riddell introduced plastic headgear that
provided a protective seal for the ram's horns.

Tank Younger and the Bull Elephants

Paul Lawrence "Tank" Younger was the first NFL player from a predominantly African-American university. He was the perfect candidate for that unique challenge. Younger was born in rural Grambling, Louisiana, and attended school and college there, but he was not a fledgling country farmer in coveralls and high-button shoes when he came to the Los Angeles Rams in 1949. In fact Younger arrived with the football cleats he wore in college— and they almost betrayed him.

Battling to make the team at the final cutdown, Tank was on the field when the Rams kicked off against the New York Giants in the final preseason game in Omaha, Nebraska, in September of 1949. Running downfield, Younger discovered that one of his shoes had split at the sole. He stayed in the game, shoe flapping and the opening savaging the bottom of his foot—rookies weren't issued new footwear until they made the team.

"In those days the roster limit was thirty-two players," Younger remembered. "I was a rookie, fighting for a job. You had to play offense, defense, and special teams. If I came out of the game, I don't think I'd ever have gotten back in. There were four or five guys fighting for the same spot. Somebody would have stepped up." At halftime, his foot bleeding and tender, Younger received treatment. He taped his shoe, went back out, and won a spot on the Rams roster.

Before he passed away four days after September 11, 2001, Younger could look back on forty-six consecutive years as an NFL player, scout, and front-office executive. He starred in every one of those roles.

Younger spent thirty-two years in the employ of the Rams. His final season as a player, 1958, was with the Pittsburgh Steelers, after which he returned to Los Angeles and began a career in business and in scouting. In 1975 Younger became the first African-American assistant general manager in the NFL when he joined the San Diego Chargers. He returned to the Rams in 1988 and retired in 1995, when the club announced it was moving to St. Louis.

Tank was exposed to two worlds growing up. He spent summers in fast-paced Los Angeles, where his father, a carpenter,

Chow Time

Tank Younger not only was a great football player and an accomplished front-office executive, but he also was an acclaimed chef. His annual dinner for the club scouts was a veritable feast of steak, Southern fried chicken, okra, green beans, and mashed potatoes.

When Tank worked for San Diego, one Chargers scout, 330-pound Aubrey "Red" Phillips, always was greeted with special place setting. While the other scouts would be furnished with standard knife and fork, Tank placed a giant butcher knife in front of Phillips, who would roll up his sleeves and begin putting away the food.

had moved the family while seeking work during the Great Depression. The rest of the year, young Paul lived in slower-paced Grambling with his maternal grandmother, a strong minded woman who nurtured his probing mind educationally and socially.

Younger was a strapping 6'3" and 225 pounds when he turned out for football as a seventeen-year-old freshman at Grambling in 1945. Head coach Eddie Robinson lined up Younger at tackle, but it didn't take long to see that the big fellow's speed and size was suited for the backfield. Younger ran through, around, and, mostly, over Grambling opponents. He scored 60 touchdowns in his collegiate career and played linebacker on defense. Collie Nicholson, the school's sports information representative, coined the nickname "Tank." Nicholson thought Younger resembled a rampaging Sherman tank in full gallop.

Dan Towler, one of the Rams famed "Bull Elephants," barrels in for the score.

Grambling played only predominantly African-American colleges in the South. No blacks had played in the NFL since 1933, and no one from the many small black colleges in the South had ever set foot on an NFL field.

But World War II had ended. There was a new NFL team in Los Angeles, and Rams owner Dan Reeves ignored the NFL's unofficial "hands off" policy regarding black players. He signed former UCLA stars Kenny Washington and Woody Strode in 1946, one year before Jackie Robinson broke into baseball's major leagues with the Brooklyn Dodgers. Reeves also was the first NFL owner to employ a full-time scouting staff. Eddie Kotal, a Rams scout, took notice when Tank was named Negro college player of the year by the black *Pittsburgh Courier* newspaper in 1948.

Younger felt some additional responsibility when he signed with the Rams as a rookie free agent the following spring. Eddie Robinson stressed the point. "We're counting on you," Robinson told Younger. "If you don't make it they may never give us [the predominantly black football programs] another chance."

Tank came to the Rams at a glorious time. Los Angeles played in the NFL Championship Game each season from 1949 to 1951, they made the playoffs in 1952, and they played in the championship game in 1955. The Rams were the most explosive and glamorous team in sports. The 1950 squad averaged an astounding 294 yards a game passing, scored a record 466 points, averaged almost 39 points a game, and had games in which they scored 70 and 65 points, including 44 points in one quarter.

It was during the 1950 season that Younger, then 235 pounds, teamed in the same backfield with 220-pound Dan

Towler and 230-pound Dick Hoerner. This supersized alignment became known as the "Bull Elephant Backfield," still one of the most famous appellations in sports. (It was coined by *Los Angeles Daily News* columnist Ned Cronin.) The Rams' smaller, niftier backs were known as the "Pony Backfield."

The Bull Elephants possibly were born of necessity. "The idea came during the 1950 season," said Towler, who died five weeks before Younger in 2001. Towler recalled that the Rams were playing a game in rainy conditions on a muddy field in Green Bay. "The coaches alternated backfields hoping to rest us. Joe [head coach Joe Stydahar] then realized he had three fullbacks of equal running ability and saw what a powerful weapon he would have with two big guys lead blocking for a third."

Rams Hall of Fame end Elroy Hirsch related the more popular version of the Elephants' birth to Stanley Grosshandler of the *Coffin Corner* football publication in 1987: "There was a quirk in the schedule," said Hirsch. "We played San Francisco two weeks in a row, and they clobbered us in the first game. The 49ers inserted two quick defensive backs [Jim Powers and Verl Lillywhite] as linebackers to stop our swift halfbacks as they came around end or deployed into the passing game." The stratagem worked when the 49ers scored an unlikely 44–17 blowout victory at Kezar Stadium.

The following week the teams met again in the Los Angeles Coliseum. To take advantage of White and Powers's lack of bulk, Stydahar employed Hoerner, Younger, and Towler, who responded with power running and nasty sweeps that bowled over the lighter defenders.

When 49ers coach Buck Shaw countered with larger, harder-hitting Don "Boom Boom" Burke and Norm Standlee at linebacker, Stydahar volleyed with the Rams' "Pony Backs"—Verda "Vitamin T" Smith, Jerry Williams, Tommy "Cricket" Kalmanir, and Glenn Davis, the erstwhile "Mr. Inside" of Army and Heisman Trophy glory. The Rams defeated the 49ers 23–16, stayed with their big backfield the rest of the season, and went on to win the NFL championship, their only title while in Los Angeles.

Younger made his first of three consecutive Pro Bowl appearances after the 1951 season. Still playing linebacker, he was a first team all-pro selection on defense. From 1951 to 1957 Younger either led the Rams or ranked among the top three Rams in rushing. His per-carry averages of 4.8 yards for his career and 6.7 yards in 1954 still rank among the club's all-time leaders.

Towler was a twenty-fifth-round draft selection in 1950 and held the Rams record for career rushing average (5.2 yards per carry) when he retired from football at age twenty-seven in 1955 to pursue a career in the ministry. "Deacon Dan" played long before David "Deacon" Jones, a great Rams defensive player of the following generation.

Towler had an impressive football pedigree. He was a star running back on the 1945 Donora High squad that rolled over other teams in football-crazy western Pennsylvania, and his academic bent took him to Washington & Jefferson, where he caught the eye of the vigilant Rams scouting department.

Towler eventually earned a doctorate in theology and was a professor at Cal State–Los Angeles. His Daniel Towler Foundation helped many youngsters realize their educational dreams.

Towler was never far away from the football field after retirement. For forty-plus years, he could be found in the Coliseum press box on Saturdays at USC or UCLA games and on Sundays

Tank Younger speaks with Herschel Walker (right) at their enshrinement into the College Football Hall of Fame in 2000.

at Rams games, working as a representative for one of the national wire services.

The frenzy of the modern Super Bowl was not lost on Towler, who regularly attended the game. "Compared to all this, 1951 was like a high school championship game," he said when the Rams advanced to Super Bowl XXXIV after the 1999 season. "The Super Bowl," Towler pontificated, "has become a sports circus, with the game almost secondary to the commercials and all that."

It was a lot different when the Rams beat the Cleveland Browns for the 1951 title. After that game, "We all got into our used cars, if we had a car, and drove home and started thinking about going to work on Monday," said Woodley Lewis, one of the five African-American Rams who played in the 1950 and 1951 championship games. "Most of us had to have other jobs." Lewis was a probation counselor.

Hoerner, the least known of the Bull Elephants, worked as an usher at Hollywood Park and Santa Anita racetracks in the off-season. Hoerner compared the Rams' individual winning share of $2,108.44 in 1951 to the $58,000 earned by the Rams players in 1999. "We were darned glad to get it," he said. "Some of the guys were playing for two thousand or three thousand dollars a year and were always drawing money against their future salary to be able to get to their homes in the off-season."

Hoerner, who was drafted by the Cleveland Rams in 1945, joined the Rams in Los Angeles in 1947. He was a punishing, inside runner who led the team in rushing in 1948 and 1949 and was a stalwart on the 1951 squad.

Hoerner's final season in 1952 was with the woeful Dallas Texans. "That team was a disgrace," he remembered. Attendance was so poor that Texans coach Jimmy Phelan suggested that players go into the stands and introduce themselves. He also cautioned them to cash their game checks immediately, fearing they would bounce. The Texans won only one game, a shocking upset of the Chicago Bears in Akron, Ohio, after they became homeless in Dallas, which forfeited the franchise to the NFL. Hoerner, who resides in La Mirada, California, was a regular visitor to the Rams offices in Anaheim after the team moved there in 1980, and he remained active with the Los Angeles chapter of the NFL alumni.

Younger stayed in football until 1995. He scouted the black colleges for the Rams and went to bat for Rams players with team executives when he felt the scales were not even.

Younger not only scouted the black colleges, he also helped nurture such all-pro players as Deacon Jones (Mississippi Valley State), Isiah Robertson (Southern), Coy Bacon (Jackson State), Willie Ellison (Texas Southern), James Harris (Grambling), and Elijah Pitts (Philander Smith).

Harold Jackson was a twelfth-round draft choice out of Jackson State in 1968, the 323rd player selected that year. Younger had scouted the slightly built, spindly receiver and was sold on his potential, a feeling not embraced by all of those involved in the team's "War Room" on draft day. Younger literally pounded the table and raised his voice to a fever pitch pushing Jackson's candidacy. Younger won, and so did the Rams. Jackson caught 579 passes and made five Pro Bowl teams in his sixteen-year career.

Younger could be direct in other situations, also. Many times Tank would be called in to give a youngster the bad news—that he was being cut from the squad. "Son," Tank would intone, "it's time for you to be getting on with your life's work."

In 1975 the San Diego Chargers were in a rebuilding mode. Team owner Gene Klein had essentially cleaned out the Chargers football department, hiring a new coaching staff in 1974 and bringing in longtime Rams scout John Sanders as his next general manager.

Klein appointed Younger assistant general manager, at the time the highest ranking football position for any African-American in the NFL. "You come back any time you want," were Rams owner Carroll Rosenbloom's parting words to Younger.

Tank went to the Chargers at the right time, although he wasn't sure how long he'd last. "We're playing Pittsburgh, the defending Super Bowl champion, in our opening game," he said. "We didn't have a player on our team who could start for the Steelers. I'm on the elevator with Gene, and he says, 'We've got to win this one!' I said, 'What, Gene? Are you kidding? We haven't got a chance.'"

Klein stared at his new assistant GM but said nothing. When the elevator reached the assigned floor, Klein headed for the owner's suite, and Tank went to the press box. Pittsburgh won 37–0, and the Chargers went on to lose eleven straight games before finishing with a 2–12 record.

San Diego improved to 6–8 in 1976, to 7–7 in 1977, to 9–7 in 1978, and to 12–4 in 1979, when they won their first division championship in fourteen years. Younger's role could never be understated. He helped foster a new, team-oriented approach among front-office employees and helped the Chargers develop a more positive profile among community leaders. Sanders and Younger usually split the duties of signing draft choices and free agents.

"Judge"

Tank Younger was a proud, contented man in retirement. I saw him a few weeks before he died. Tank was in a hospital bed at his home in Los Angeles's Lafayette Park. He was smoking one of his ritual, old-time cigarettes. "Judge, my doctor tells me of all the things wrong with me, cigarettes ain't one of them," he said. "So I'm not giving up that vice."

You knew you were accepted when Tank called you "Judge." He used it only for his friends.

It was not uncommon to hear profane, heated exchanges coming from behind Younger's office door. Usually Tank was fencing and parrying with a player agent. And usually cooler heads prevailed, the player was signed, and everyone moved on. Younger did much of the heavy lifting when the Chargers, like other NFL teams, confronted the specter of drug use by some of their players.

Younger negotiated the first million-dollar radio contract for the Chargers in 1983. It was one of the highest in the league and an incredible number for small-market San Diego. When Klein saw the contract he did a double take. "Are you sure about this?" he said. When Younger nodded, Klein's razorlike business sense kicked in. "This is great, but let's squeeze 'em a little."

The great run in San Diego began to end when Klein sold the team in 1984. Younger left the Chargers after the 1987 season and returned to the Rams, for whom he picked up many of his former duties. Younger could have gone with the Rams to St. Louis in 1995, but he chose to retire instead. He wanted to spend time enjoying the company of his wife, children, and grandchildren.

Hooray for Hollywood

Television was just dawning in the late 1940s, promising to thrust the National Football League into America's living room, but that was not the only medium that would make the Los Angeles Rams one of the NFL's most recognized franchises. The arrival of a player named "Crazylegs" helped. Elroy Hirsch was known as Crazylegs because of the wild, splaying action of his feet on the football field. *Chicago Daily News* sportswriter Francis Powers spawned the nickname when he wrote about Hirsch following a University of Wisconsin game in 1942. In that game Hirsch scored on a 61-yard touchdown run while playing for the Badgers against the Great Lakes Navy team at Soldier Field. "His crazy legs were gyrating in six different directions, all at the same time," Powers wrote. "He looked like a demented duck!"

One of Hirsch's Rams quarterbacks, Norm Van Brocklin, put it this way in 1951: "Talk about the gent who zigged when he should have zagged, 'Roy also has a zog and a couple varieties of zug when he's under full steam."

Hirsch came to the Rams as a running back in 1949 and rocketed to star status in the Rams' revolutionary "three-end" offense in 1950. Flanked from the line of scrimmage, Hirsch became football's first true wide receiver. He set an NFL record in 1951 by catching 17 touchdown passes, with 10 of them covering distances of more than 40 yards. That same year the NFL Championship Game was nationally televised for the first time. The Rams defeated the Cleveland Browns 24–17.

Crazylegs's popularity helped elevate the Rams' profile throughout the country, and Hollywood was quick to notice. Tall, athletic, and handsome, Hirsch was clearly movie material. He starred in two films, *Crazylegs, All-American* in 1953 and *Unchained* in 1955, and he had a key supporting role in *Zero Hour* in 1957.

Hirsch wasn't the first football player or the first Rams star to go Hollywood, but he was one of the few to earn critical acclaim. Generally the plots and performances in football movies were, well, not up to Academy Award standards.

Elroy Hirsch's crazy legs carried him to the Pro Football Hall of Fame.

The film capital has had an affinity for football players and football themes dating to the era of silent movies. The first of this genre probably was *One Minute to Play*. Made in 1926 it featured Red Grange, the "Galloping Ghost," from the University of Illinois and the Chicago Bears and the biggest name of the era in football. Grange, playing the role of Red Wade, shook off an injury, came into the game with one minute to play, and scored the winning touchdown.

Many low-budget productions involving football players followed Grange's foray into Hollywood. Rams players took participation to a new level after the franchise moved to Los Angeles in 1946. "We became part of the Hollywood crowd," said tackle Gil Bouley. "We even had to get cards from the Screen Actors Guild."

Fred Gehrke and nearly all of his teammates were in the 1949 drama *Easy Living*. A star player for the New York Chiefs, played by Victor Mature, had a heart condition that he attempted to keep from the team. Lucille Ball, Sonny Tufts, Lloyd Nolan, and Jack Paar also were in the movie, with Paar playing the role of a reporter named Scoop Spooner.

Gehrke had a two-line speaking part. During a gin rummy game on a railroad trip, Gehrke offered a deck of cards to Ms. Ball and said, "Cut 'em for luck, Anne." Gehrke also leveled Mature during football practice, provoking a dirty look from the coach. "I didn't block him, Coach, I only brushed him," Gehrke replied. Other thankfully forgotten lines from the film included: "Love's not like football, baby . . . one fumble and you're through," and "I hate to see him kick her heart around like it was just a football."

Tom Harmon, who played for the Rams in 1946 and 1947, parlayed the movies into a long career in broadcasting. Harmon starred in 1941's *Harmon of Michigan*, which quickly recapped his Heisman Trophy year at Michigan, then deteriorated into a fictitious account of his career as an unethical coach. Harmon's most important role, professionally and personally, was in 1946's *The Sweetheart of Sigma Chi*. Harmon played Elyse Knox's rowing coach in the film, then married Knox in real life and fathered actors Mark Harmon and Kelly Harmon. He also was the father-in-law of singer Ricky Nelson, who had first been introduced to television as the young son on *Ozzie and Harriet*.

Rams quarterback Bob Waterfield played football player Bob Miller in *Jungle Manhunt* in 1951. Lost in the jungle, Miller was found by Jungle Jim, who was played by Johnny Weissmuller, the former Olympic swimmer who also was the original motion picture *Tarzan*. (Rams linebacker Mike Henry didn't immediately succeed Weissmuller, but he became the movies' new Tarzan in the 1960s.)

Another Rams lineman, Harry Thompson, was cast in 1954 as Nubian, a palace functionary holding a leash to restrain a leopard in *The Egyptian*. The movie was bluntly described by one critic as a "sword-and-sandal, ponderous, big-budget epic about a young Egyptian in Aknaton's epoch who becomes physician to the Pharaoh."

Hirsch, however, was different from most football-players-turned-actor. He played significant roles and displayed star quality in front of the camera. Online entertainment columnist Ron Miller wrote after Hirsch passed away at age eighty early in 2004: "He started out as the main star in his first movie,

Tom Harmon during his college
playing days at Michigan.

Crazylegs, because it was all about his football career. It's highly unusual for the movies to actually do what's known as a 'biopic,' while the athlete still is active in the game . . . ." Lobby posters of *Crazylegs* heralded the presence in the cast of "Los Angeles Rams Negro stars" Tank Younger, Woodley Lewis, Dan Towler, and Dick "Night Train" Lane. Actor Lloyd Nolan played Hirsch's coach, and Joan Vohs was a love interest.

Former USC All-America Irvine "Cotton" Warburton, who, like many other Trojans and UCLA Bruins had gravitated to Hollywood after their playing careers, received an Academy Award nomination for the editing of *Crazylegs*. Warburton won an Academy Award ten years later for his work on *Mary Poppins*. Hirsch's producer was Hall Bartlett, who directed Elroy in his second movie, *Unchained*.

In *Unchained*, a fact-based story filmed at the correctional facility in Chino, California, Hirsch played the role of Steve Davitt, a prison inmate dealing with "the division of one man's soul . . . part of him wants to continue his criminal ways and attempt to escape, while the other half wants to get home to his wife and family." In this movie, Hirsch "turns in a surprisingly inspired performance," according to one review.

Released by Warner Brothers in 1955, *Unchained* also featured a title song, "Unchained Melody," which Al Hibbler and Roy Hamilton made into a hit record that year. It was made more famous in the 1960s, however, by the Righteous Brothers, whose haunting rendition also was heard many years later in the Whoopi Goldberg–Demi Moore–Patrick Swayze classic film, *Ghost*.

Hirsch was thirty-two in 1955 when he considered retiring from football to pursue a full-time acting career. He stayed with the Rams two more years, though, retiring after the 1957 season, secure with Pro Football Hall of Fame credentials. He caught 387 passes for 7,029 yards and 60 touchdowns. His 1951 season remains perhaps the greatest ever for a wide receiver. In just twelve games, Crazylegs caught 66 passes for 1,495 yards and 17 touchdowns. Projected over today's sixteen-game NFL schedule, Hirsch's totals would have been 88 catches, 1,993 yards (a record), and 23 touchdowns (another record).

In his final season as a player, Hirsch starred in *Zero Hour*, sharing top billing with Dana Andrews, Linda Darnell, and Sterling Hayden. Hirsch was Captain Bill Wilson, pilot of an airliner on which passengers and crew become critically ill with food poisoning.

Retired and enjoying lunches at Scandia Restaurant, his favorite haunt on Hollywood's Sunset Boulevard, Hirsch suddenly became the Rams general manager after Pete Rozelle was named the NFL commissioner in 1960. He was instrumental in the 1966 appointment of head coach George Allen, who led the Rams to a division championship in 1967 and brought them out of a half-decade malaise during which the team's record was 23–56–4.

Hirsch returned to the University of Wisconsin as the school's athletic director in 1969. The Badgers' combined record in the two previous seasons was 0–19–1. The athletic department faced a $200,000 budget deficit. John Maturi, a high school coach in Madison, remembered how Hirsch immediately began working to rekindle interest in the Badgers athletic programs. "I

Crazylegs

Here are Elroy Hirsch's career pass-catching statistics:

YEAR	TEAM	NO	YDS	AVG	TDS
1946	Chicago Rockets	27	347	12.9	3
1947	Chicago Rockets	10	282	28.2	3
1948	Chicago Rockets	7	101	14.4	1
1949	L.A. Rams	22	326	14.8	4
1950	L.A. Rams	42	687	16.4	7
1951	L.A. Rams	66	1,495	22.7	17
1952	L.A. Rams	25	590	23.6	4
1953	L.A. Rams	61	941	15.4	4
1954	L.A. Rams	35	720	20.6	3
1955	L.A. Rams	25	460	18.4	2
1956	L.A. Rams	35	603	17.2	6
1957	L.A. Rams	32	477	14.9	6
Totals		387	7,029	18.2	60

think Elroy visited every high school in the state of Wisconsin," said Maturi, who is now the athletic director at the University of Minnesota. "I don't know of anyone who had the passion for Wisconsin athletics like Elroy did."

It was in Hirsch's native Wausau, Wisconsin, that he began the curious odyssey that would eventually land him in Los Angeles with the Rams. After a legendary high school career, Hirsch played only one season at the University of Wisconsin, amassing more than 1,000 yards rushing, receiving, and passing and leading the Badgers to a 8–1–1 record in 1942.

Rams star Woody Strode (right) squared off with Kirk Douglas in Spartacus.

After enlisting in the Marine Corps, a commitment to the Navy's V-12 program required Hirsch to report to the University of Michigan for basic training in June of 1943. School officials also found time to get him into the Wolverines athletic programs. Hirsch played one season at Michigan, leading the Wolverines to the Big Ten championship and an 8–1 record in 1943. He also became the only athlete in school history to letter in four sports: football, basketball, baseball, and track. Although selected by the Rams in the first round of the 1945 NFL draft, Hirsch's military commitment precluded his joining the pros until 1946.

As the defending NFL champions, the Rams were preparing to play in the annual Chicago College All-Star Game against a group of collegiate stars in 1946. A signing war between the NFL and the newly formed All-America Football Conference already was under way. The new league was flexing its muscle. Forty-four of the sixty All-Stars eventually signed with AAFC teams. Hirsch would be among them.

Hirsch led the College All-Stars to a surprise win over the Rams. He also signed with the AAFC's Chicago Rockets, big news in the All-Stars training camp but no coincidence. Hirsch had most recently played for the Marine Corps team in El Toro, California. Hirsch's El Toro coach was Dick Hanley, who became coach of the Rockets.

Hirsch recalled his three seasons with Chicago as "frightful." The Rockets were the AAFC's most disappointing franchise. Hanley lost control of the team early and was fired three games into the 1946 season. Chicago Bears quarterback Sid Luckman declined an offer to be head coach. Three veteran players more or less coached the squad for the next five games, then they turned responsibility over to one of the team's original assistant coaches.

The Rockets were 1–13 in 1947, as Hirsch was in and out of the lineup with injuries. Early in another 1–13 season in 1948, Hirsch carried the ball into the line on a running play and suffered a fractured skull that sidelined him the rest of the year, prompting fear that he never would play again.

Elroy joined the Rams when his contract with the Rockets expired after the 1948 season. Bill Granholm, Elroy's lifelong friend from Wausau, also moved to the Rams from Chicago as the club's equipment manager. Granholm helped devise a special protective helmet Hirsch would wear for the remainder of his playing days.

When Hirsch retired as a player, Hollywood was in a period during which there was little interest in football movies or in football players. Burt Reynolds and *The Longest Yard* revived the football movie genre in 1974, but it remained for the Rams to be the focus in perhaps the best of all football movies.

Warren Beatty starred in *Heaven Can Wait*, which was released in 1978. Beatty played Rams quarterback Joe Pendleton, who is killed in an accident but comes back to life in the body of a recently murdered multimillionaire. Joe then buys the Rams so he can play quarterback, and he leads them to the Super Bowl. An outstanding cast, including Julie Christie, James

Mason, Dyan Cannon, Charles Grodin, and Jack Warden, was joined by Rams players such as Deacon Jones, Jack Snow, and Charlie Cowan.

The Golden Age

In prose and in poetry, the decade of the 1950s has been honored as pro football's "Golden Age." Television was bringing to America the fast, hard-hitting NFL, complete with its assortment of hardscrabble characters and stevedore personalities. You had to be tough to play the game. The modern face mask had not yet come to pro football. Black eyes, broken noses, excavated teeth, and fractured mandibles were not uncommon.

For the Los Angeles Rams, the Golden Age began in 1949, when the struggling All-America Football Conference disbanded at season's end. The AAFC's Los Angeles Dons, who had been a formidable, imaginative opponent for the Rams in competition for the hearts of the area's football fans (and for the windfall of the gate receipts), went the way of that league.

As late as 1948, the AAFC's third season, the Dons were gaining traction, drawing more fans to the Los Angeles Coliseum than the Rams. Buttressed by membership in the established NFL, the Rams averaged 42,474 fans for six home games in 1946, while the first-year Dons drew an average of just 20,916. In 1947, though, the Dons averaged 43,453 to the Rams' 33,145. The following year the Dons' average was 40,050 to the Rams' 31,680.

Were it not for big crowds against the champion Chicago Cardinals in 1947 and the Chicago Bears in 1948, the Rams would have been further behind the Dons in this annual attendance firefight. But then the AAFC began dropping teams and losing its identity. The Dons' attendance fell off to an average of 22,064 in their last season in 1949, while the Rams, thanks to a 6–0 start and their first Western Conference championship, jumped to 49,855.

The Rams capped their six-game winning streak with a 27–24 win over the Chicago Bears before 86,080 fans, a record NFL regular season crowd at the time. However, they won only two of their final six games and finished the year with an 8–2–2 mark. Despite a 53–27 win over the comatose Washington Redskins in the final game of the regular season, the Rams were not exactly on a roll going into the championship game against the Philadelphia Eagles.

The Rams, anticipating another big crowd, were disheartened by a winter rainstorm that soaked Southern California.

Only 22,000-plus were on hand to witness the Eagles' Steve Van Buren slosh to a title game record 196 yards rushing as the Eagles won 14–0. Rams owner Dan Reeves fired head coach Clark Shaughnessy and elevated assistant coach Joe Stydahar.

Historians have praised Shaughnessy for having one of the game's most creative minds. As a part-time consultant for the Chicago Bears, he was instrumental in the installation of the modern T-formation with which the Bears won three straight NFL championships from 1940 to 1942, including their record-breaking 73–0 rout over the Redskins in 1940.

In 1940 Shaughnessy became head coach at Stanford University, which was 1–7–1 in 1939. Utilizing the T behind sure-handed quarterback Frankie Albert, the "Wow Boys" of Stanford were 9–0 in the regular season and defeated Nebraska 21–13 in the 1941 Rose Bowl.

Shaughnessy joined the Rams as an assistant coach in 1947 and replaced Bob Snyder as head coach a year later. In 1949 Shaughnessy installed his "three-end" system, which put the Rams in the vanguard of NFL offenses. However, the coach was a peevish taskmaster, the kind players usually dislike. And to Reeves's consternation, Shaughnessy could be abrasive and condescending in one-on-one meetings with the owner.

The new coach, "Jumbo" Joe Stydahar, a former lineman with the Chicago Bears' "Monsters of the Midway," accelerated Shaughnessy's three-end offense. In this alignment halfback Elroy Hirsch was flanked outside tight end Jack Zilly and was a step behind the line of scrimmage. Tom Fears was the split end on the other side. This new formation eventually was adopted by all teams, but none with the success of the Rams, who scored 64 touchdowns in twelve games in 1950.

Figures can be misleading. At least that was the situation with the Rams home attendance. The club averaged only 26,804 fans for six games. The Rams made history, however, by becoming the first team to have both home and away games televised. Reeves entered into an agreement in which sponsor Admiral Television Company reimbursed the Rams when the gate fell below a predetermined figure. At the end of the season, the sponsor had a large bill for empty seats. Reeves scored a profit, and the television exposure converted many viewers into Rams fans.

So it was no surprise that the Rams' popularity increased. The 1950 team set offensive standards that still resonate, including an all-time league best of 38.8 points per game during the regular season. Hirsch, Fears, and quarterbacks Bob Waterfield and Norm Van Brocklin all are now in the Pro Football Hall of Fame.

The Rams reached the championship game again in 1950 but not before a season-long battle with the Bears that resulted in a tie in the standings and necessitated a conference playoff—the first since 1941. The Bears had beaten the Rams 24–20 and 24–14 in the regular season—a sweep that would have given Chicago the conference title under current tiebreaking procedures but not under those of the era.

Waterfield and Van Brocklin alternated playing time during the year, prompting pro football's first quarterback controversy. Both quarterbacks would be selected to the Pro Bowl, which was making a comeback for the first time since the game was canceled because of World War II in 1942. Waterfield was named the NFL's most valuable player for 1950 by the Washington Touchdown Club. Van Brocklin passed for 18 touchdowns in 233 attempts; Waterfield had 11 touchdown passes in his 215 attempts. The two of them even split punting chores.

There was no question who would start against the Bears, however. Stydahar nominated Van Brocklin. In the days leading up to the game, Waterfield was at home in Sherman Oaks, California, with actress-wife Jane Russell nursing her husband through a 103-degree temperature and the effects of the flu. Waterfield still was feeling weak and feverish the day before the game. On Sunday he was driven to the Coliseum by his wife and prepared to serve in a backup role. He still did not feel well.

A crowd of 83,501 filed into the Coliseum on a warm, hazy December afternoon. When a Rams drive in the first quarter stalled at the Bears' 35 yard line, Waterfield came off the bench to kick a 43-yard field goal.

The Bears, pounding the ball with backs George Gulyanics, Julie Rykovich, and Fred "Curly" Morrison, took a 7–3 lead in the second quarter. Van Brocklin, who was hit hard and sustained a broken rib early in the game, threw 8 consecutive incompletions. Stydahar looked at Waterfield, who began to loosen up on the sidelines.

Waterfield came onto the field in the second quarter and entered the Rams huddle, at which point he promptly threw up. Gathering himself, the thirty-year-old veteran went to work. Waterfield hit Fears on a 68-yard touchdown pass play and on a 27-yard pass to give the Rams a 17–7 lead at halftime. Waterfield found Fears again for a 22-yard touchdown in the third quarter, and the Rams were home free. They went on to win 24–14.

It was a remarkable performance by the ailing Waterfield. He completed 14 of 21 passes for 298 yards, kicked a field goal and three points-after-touchdown, and kept the Bears pinned in their end of the field with 6 punts that averaged 46 yards. Fears, who set an NFL record with 84 receptions during the regular season—

including 18 in one game to set a single-game record that would stand for half a century—caught 7 passes for 198 yards.

Waterfield got the start in Cleveland in the championship game. It was played in chilly Christmas Eve weather, with snow flurries and a cold wind blowing in from Lake Erie that augmented the 20-degree temperature at kickoff. Waterfield struck with Glenn Davis for an 82-yard touchdown pass on the first play from scrimmage.

The game turned into a brutal struggle. Rams fullback Dick Hoerner gouged his way for 83 yards in 24 carries and scored 2 touchdowns against the Browns' strong defense. Waterfield, though he was intercepted four times, passed for 312 yards and had the Rams in front 28–20 entering the fourth quarter.

No lead was safe against the NFL newcomer Browns. Following the 1949 season Cleveland had been merged into the league with the Baltimore Colts and the San Francisco 49ers after the AAFC folded. That league collapsed in no small measure because of the talent of the Browns and their quarter-back Otto Graham, who had led them to a combined record of 51–4–3 and four consecutive championships.

There was some sneering by provincial honks when the Browns came into the NFL, but that was quieted quickly when Cleveland hammered the 1949 champion Philadelphia Eagles 35–10 in the opening game of the 1950 season. The NFL was taken aback by Graham's precise, accurate passes and his tough, get-down scrambling ability.

In the title game against the Rams, Graham completed 22 of 32 passes for 298 yards and 4 touchdowns, and he ran twelve times for 99 yards. With his team trailing by 8 points in the final period, Graham marshaled two long drives. He brought the

Otto Graham (60) led Cleveland to a 30–28 victory over the Rams in the 1950 championship.

Browns within 1 point of the Rams by completing 9 passes in a row, 5 of them to Dante Lavelli, and concluding with a 14-yard touchdown pass to Rex Baumgardner. Cleveland got the ball back again with two minutes remaining, and Graham marched them to Lou Groza's 22-yard field goal with 28 seconds left on the clock. The Browns won 30–28.

Despite the loss the Rams were a young team, talented, hungry, and believing in future greatness. Eight Rams—Waterfield, Van Brocklin, Fears, Davis, Hoerner, tackle Dick Huffman,

Scoring Machine

The Rams averaged 38.8 points per game during the 1950 regular season. That established an NFL record that still stands more than half a century later. Here's how they did it:

DATE	RAMS	OPPONENT	
Sept. 17	20	Chicago Bears	24
Sept. 22	45	New York Yankees	28
Oct. 1	35	at San Francisco	14
Oct. 8	20	at Philadelphia	56
Oct. 15	30	at Detroit	28
Oct. 22	70	Baltimore	27
Oct. 29	65	Detroit	24
Nov. 5	28	San Francisco	21
Nov. 12	45	at Green Bay	14
Nov. 19	43	at New York Yankees	35
Nov. 26	14	at Chicago Bears	24
Dec. 3	51	Green Bay	14
(9–3–0)	466		309

defensive end Larry Brink, and defensive back Woodley Lewis—made the Pro Bowl that season.

Stydahar attempted to strengthen his lines by drafting guard Bud McFadin of Texas in the first round of the 1951 draft, then he selected tackle Charley Toogood of Nebraska in the third round. He also came up with guard Dick Daugherty of Oregon in the eighteenth round and defensive end Andy Robustelli of tiny Arnold College in Connecticut in the nineteenth round.

Norm Van Brocklin (left) and Tom Fears celebrate their playoff game victory over Cleveland in 1951.

Robustelli, a Ram from 1951 to 1955, would go on to a Pro Football Hall of Fame career with the New York Giants.

The Rams still relied on their big-play weapons, but the season's first two games provided an eerie contrast. The Rams opened the season in New York against the not-so-aptly named Yankees. Van Brocklin passed for 554 yards, and the Rams gained 735 total yards, both still NFL records, in a 54–14 victory. Van Brocklin completed 27 of 41 passes to eight different receivers. Elroy "Crazylegs" Hirsch caught 4 touchdown passes.

The following week, the Rams were spanked in their home opener, falling 38–23 to the defending champion Browns before a crowd of 67,186 at the Coliseum. The Browns ran right at the Rams, gaining 307 yards on the ground. Marion Motley rushed for 106 yards on 13 carries, and Dub Jones had 110 yards on 15 carries. Graham added 219 yards passing. In the span of one week, the Rams had gained 735 yards, then given up 526.

The Browns still were the best in the NFL, although a new power was emerging in the Western Conference. The Detroit Lions, behind swashbuckling quarterback Bobby Layne, dropped a 27–21 decision to the Rams in week 3 but beat them 24–22 in week 11. That win pulled Detroit a half game ahead of the Rams heading into the final week.

Two successive games on the West Coast proved too much for the freewheeling Lions. The Rams beat Green Bay 42–14 and San Francisco edged Detroit 21–17 on the season's final Sunday, sending the Rams to the championship game against Cleveland again.

After a scoreless first quarter, the teams battled back and forth until midway through the fourth quarter, when Van Brocklin and Fears combined on a 55-yard touchdown pass for a 24–17 Rams'

The 1951 NFL Championship Game

The Rams won their first NFL title in Los Angeles by beating the Cleveland Browns, the pro team that succeeded them when the Rams vacated Cleveland following the 1945 season, 24–17 at the Memorial Coliseum. Here's the box score from that championship game:

Cleveland	0	10	0	7—17
Los Angeles	0	7	7	10—24

LA—Hoerner 1 run (Waterfield kick)
Cle—FG Groza 52
Cle—Jones 17 pass from Graham (Groza kick)
LA—Towler 1 run (Waterfield kick)
LA—FG Waterfield 17
Cle—Carpenter 5 run (Groza kick)
LA—Fears 73 pass from Van Brocklin (Waterfield kick)

Attendance—57,522

TEAM STATISTICS	CLEVELAND	LOS ANGELES
First downs	22	20
Rushing yards	92	81
Passing yards	280	253
Total yards	372	334

victory. The Browns thought that the collision between their two defensive backs in pass coverage freed Fears, but the Rams end was quick to praise his quarterback.

"That was the best thrown pass I ever caught in my life," Fears told reporters after the game. "He laid it right in there when I was going full stride."

Breaking Up the Old Gang

The Los Angeles Rams were in transition. As they began their tenth season in California in 1955, the Rams filed into training camp 60 miles east of the city at hot, dry Redlands University, where they awaited head coach Sid Gillman's first whistle. Gillman was the Rams' sixth coach since they moved west from Cleveland in 1946, and he promised changes. A driven coach with a sharp edge, Gillman replaced the quiet, studious Hamp

Pool, whose undoing after a 6–5–1 season came amid a zany chain of events that seemed to have a cumulative effect:

■ Some Rams assistant coaches, encouraged by fans and even sportswriters, reportedly had revolted against Pool.

■ Unnamed players complained to Rams Fan Club members that Pool had "spoken too harshly" to the team at halftime of a game.

■ The coach was discovered reading Norman Vincent Peale's *The Power of Positive Thinking*, resulting in some unwelcome fun being poked in his direction.

■ The president of the Rams Booster Club, a large, vocal organization, publicly charged that quarterback Norm Van Brocklin refused to pass the ball to end Elroy "Crazylegs" Hirsch because of "personal jealousy."

Pool fired his assistants—Howard "Red" Hickey, Dick Voris, John Sauer, and Ralph Weaver—at the end of the 1954 season, but it was too late. Pool himself was dismissed, and the Rams' search led to Gillman, who had compiled a record of 81–19–2 as head coach at Miami of Ohio and the University of Cincinnati.

Fiery and willful, Gillman had picked up his share of critics and admirers over the years. At the time the Rams approached him, Gillman had recently signed a new eight-year contract at Cincinnati, although the university was on National Collegiate Athletic Association probation for a recruiting violation.

Perhaps it was sour grapes, but Cincinnati writer Earl Lawson offered this observation about the departing coach: "He antagonized many people at his own school with his tactless statements, extravagant demands on the athletic budget, and his high pressure recruiting tactics. Yes, he won games. Year by year Cincinnati moved closer to becoming one of the country's big football schools. University officials felt they were holding a hot potato—

and were afraid to drop it. Then Gillman took the school off the hook by leaving."

With the security of an extended contract at Cincinnati, Gillman didn't jump at the Rams' first offer. He went so far as to tell Rams owner Dan Reeves, "I am not to be considered a candidate for this job." The coach announced to the Cincinnati media: "I'm glad I'm out from under that . . . I've got a job to do, and it's right here." The Rams and Gillman then settled on a four-year contract four days later.

"Several coaching friends advised me not to take the Los Angeles job," Gillman told Mel Durslag of the *Los Angeles Examiner*. "One of them said to me, 'Everything is wild out there.'"

A Midwesterner from Minneapolis who was an All-America end at Ohio State and who had hoped to become that university's head coach (Woody Hayes got the job), the forty-four-year-old Gillman cited his reasons for going to Los Angeles: "It paid more money than I was earning at Cincinnati," he said. "More important it was a chance at last for me to prove myself in the toughest competition in sports, the National Football League. There's as much difference between college football and pro as checkers and chess, and I had confidence in myself as a chess player."

"We were impressed by his record and what other coaches said," Reeves revealed. "We found that he was an extremely intense, enthusiastic, and determined individual who was thoroughly convinced of his own ability."

Gillman soon found the Los Angeles media, with its five daily newspapers, and Rams fans to be a pesky bunch, much like similar groups in Ohio, only much larger. To introduce the new coach, the Rams arranged an informal reception at a hotel. "I assumed this was a social function and came prepared to shake a few hands

Sid Gillman at his induction into the
Pro Football Hall of Fame.

and drink a couple martinis," Sid recalled. "Before I could get my bearings, the questions came fast and furious. 'Did I feel it was important to win preseason games? Did I plan to call the plays? Why didn't my teams at Cincinnati throw more passes?'"

The Rams Booster Club, an organization with no certified clout but obvious ability to be heard, provided the new coach with a clear understanding of what to expect when he attended a luncheon. "It was only the middle of June," said Gillman, "far ahead of the season, but there were 650 people there. I was amazed by such a crowd at that time of year."

After speaking briefly Gillman invited questions from the audience. According to Durslag, one fan stood up and asked with grave concern, "If Hugh McElhenny [the great San Francisco 49ers running back] caught a screen pass and started to run, how would you defense him downfield?" "I'd probably get a gun and shoot him," replied Gillman, smiling at his own joke. The fan didn't find this funny and persisted. "Do you mean you're not going to have defensive protection downfield?" he asked. "Once he catches the pass and gets beyond the scrimmage line, there isn't much I can do, is there?" said Gillman, trying to stay cool. "I'm going to try and arrange it so he doesn't get beyond the line of scrimmage." Visibly upset and not satisfied, the fan finally sat down. Gillman winced, beginning to wonder if he hadn't been hasty in leaving Cincinnati.

There were other hurdles for the NFL rookie and his associates. "The Rams had a lot of veterans who weren't happy that none of us had coached on the professional level," said Jack Faulkner, an assistant on Gillman's first staff in 1955. "It was a tense get-acquainted period for a lot of us."

A 3–0 start helped ease things, but Gillman was beginning to turn the team over. Billy Wade saw playing time behind Norm

Trading Places

The Rams have been involved in four of the six biggest trades (based on the number of players or draft choices involved) in NFL history. Here are the largest trades in league history:

18 players (1989): **Minnesota acquired running back Herschel Walker and four draft choices from the Dallas Cowboys in exchange for five players and eight picks.**

15 players (1953): **The Baltimore Colts traded five players to the Cleveland Browns in exchange for ten players. Among the players the Colts received was Don Shula, who went on to greater fame as the club's head coach (and later as coach for the Miami Dolphins).**

15 players (1971): **The Rams acquired linebacker Marlin McKeever and seven draft choices in exchange for six players and a draft pick.**

12 players (1952): **The Rams acquired the selection rights to linebacker Les Richter in exchange for eleven players.**

10 players (1959): **The Rams acquired halfback Ollie Matson from the Chicago Cardinals in exchange for eight players and a draft choice.**

10 players (1987): **The Rams sent running back Eric Dickerson to the Indianapolis Colts in a three-way deal that also involved the Buffalo Bills.**

Van Brocklin at quarterback. Dan Towler, who would retire at the end of the season to pursue a career in the ministry, was being phased out at fullback. Elroy Hirsch seriously considered retiring after some success as a movie actor.

The Rams posted an 8–3–1 record to win the Western Conference for the fourth time in seven years, but their offense averaged just 334 yards a game, down from an average of 406 yards since 1949. Their defense improved marginally. It was hard to complain with Gillman's initial success, but second-guessing seemed to come from every corner of Southern California.

The Rams were no match for quarterback Otto Graham and the Cleveland Browns in the 1955 NFL Championship Game. Graham, a future hall of famer who was playing in his last game, passed for 2 touchdowns and ran for 2 more as the Browns silenced a crowd of almost 86,000 in the Coliseum with a 38–14 victory. Cleveland led 38–7 in the fourth quarter. Van Brocklin was intercepted 6 times.

The following year started poorly and got worse. A dispute between managing partner Dan Reeves and partners Edwin Pauley, Hal Seley, and Fred Levy continued to build steam. On June 18, 1956, Reeves declined to buy out his partners and asked a Los Angeles Superior Court judge to dissolve the partnership. For years it was not generally known that Reeves, after sustaining financial losses almost yearly, sold two-thirds of his ownership to Pauley, Levy, and Seley in 1947. On May 27, 1956, just weeks before Reeves went to court, Pauley had proposed that Reeves either buy the partners' two-thirds interest for $2 million or sell them his one-third interest for $1 million.

The Rams beat Philadelphia 27–7 to open the 1956 season but then lost eight of their next nine games and finished in a tie for sixth in the West with a 4–8 record. Tom Fears, a hero of the 1951 championship, announced his retirement before the final game after catching only 5 passes all season. Wade and Van Brocklin alternated at quarterback. Van Brocklin, who was naturally acerbic and cantankerous, was not happy. Wade clearly had more playing time, throwing more passes (178 attempts to Van Brocklin's 124) for more yards (1,461 to 966) and more touchdowns (10 to 7).

The quarterbacks were polar opposites. Wade was a polite, earnest young man from Vanderbilt University in his hometown of Nashville, Tennessee. "I did things a lot different from Van Brocklin," said Wade. "He had his methods, which I didn't always agree with, and I had mine."

Gillman reflected on the disastrous season: "I had decided I would alternate my two quarterbacks, which was a frightful error. The two-quarterback system rarely proves as satisfactory as one man's handling the job. A quarterback running the team has to have the feeling that the bench is behind him." Gillman was aware of Van Brocklin's strong will. "To be at his best he must be number one at all times," said the coach.

Another more incendiary situation involved Gillman's decision to call the plays. He utilized a "messenger guard" to bring in instructions from the bench. The practice originated in Cleveland, where Browns coach Paul Brown sent plays to the field via alternating offensive linemen. This was okay when Wade was in the game, but Van Brocklin chafed under the restraint. Coaches calling plays was still relatively new in football, and the decision opened Gillman to another round of second guesses and criticism.

In those days it was traditional for a coach to bring players to the weekly booster club luncheon. The media covered the event, which began with questions from the audience after lunch. At one of the sessions, guard Duane Putnam got this inquiry: "Why don't you put out on your blocks for Wade as you do for Van Brocklin?" Gillman erupted. "That's a mean insinuation," he said, leveling his gaze at the interrogator. "Duane happens to be the most conscientious team player in football."

Running back Tom Wilson was asked, "Why doesn't Gillman play you more?" Wilson wanted more playing time, but it was an embarrassing question. Wilson finally replied, "I guess the coach is playing his best men." Tackle Charley Toogood was asked, "Who do you think should call signals, the coach or quarterback?" Toogood, who was traded after the season, poured kerosene on the fire. "When the quarterback calls 'em, we feel freer to make suggestions," he said.

The fan club also had a women's auxiliary, which met with the coach once a season. One woman challenged Sid with, "Why do you treat Van Brocklin like Charlie McCarthy? Aren't you jeopardizing his job by calling the plays?" "Lady," Gillman responded icily, "he could be jeopardizing mine." Gillman's reaction reduced the woman to tears. He felt awful.

An intellectual man with great command of the language, Gillman did not suffer fools easily. He was also ahead of his time, because eventually all NFL coaches called the plays. Gillman learned to harness his emotions more or less at public gatherings. Soon no matter how absurd or naive the question, the coach often would reply, "Your idea merits consideration. We'll take it up at the next staff meeting."

For 1957 there were two major differences in the organizational makeup. Pete Rozelle, the team's director of public relations in the early 1950s, returned from a job with a San Francisco public relations firm to serve as the club's general manager and as its liaison between Reeves and the other owners. General manager Tex Schramm, tired of the bickering, resigned to take a position with the Columbia Broadcasting System in New York. Gillman, meanwhile, gave the ball back to Van Brocklin, with one caveat. The coach would call the plays.

"My nine years with the Rams were happy and prosperous," said Van Brocklin in 1961. "I probably would still be with them except for a delicate situation involving coach Sid Gillman and myself. We both wanted to call the signals, Gillman from the sidelines the way Paul Brown does at Cleveland. I thought I could call the plays better from my position back of the center." Such tact surprised even Van Brocklin's closest friends.

The Rams moved quickly to establish momentum in 1957. They defeated the Southern California All-Stars 84–0 to begin a 6–1 preseason. That was followed by a 63–21 rout of the Chicago Cardinals, a 58–27 mauling of the 49ers, and a victory over the Browns.

After a 17–13 win over the Philadelphia Eagles in the regular season opener, the Rams lost three straight games on the road and fell out of contention. They rallied to finish with a 6–6 record, and there were reasons to feel optimistic about the future.

Following years of indifferent success in the collegiate draft, the Rams had scored in 1957 with first-round choices Jon Arnett of USC and Del Shofner of Baylor; second-round selections Jack Pardee of Texas A & M and Billy Ray Smith of Arkansas; and fourth-round pick Lamar Lundy of Purdue. All eventually had long, distinguished careers in the NFL.

While the team didn't go anywhere in the NFL's Western Conference, it traveled in style. The Rams averaged 74,296 fans

Jaguar Jon

The Rams staggered out of the blocks in 1958 and were just 2–3 after five games. But a star was born the following week. "Jaguar" Jon Arnett was perfect for the role. Handsome and athletic, Arnett had grace and explosion on the football field and had married a Rose Parade princess. He attended Manual Arts High, located 2 blocks from the Coliseum and its next-door neighbor, USC.

There were 100,740 fans in that Coliseum on November 2, 1958, when the Rams took on the Chicago Bears. Arnett didn't score a touchdown, but he gained 295 yards rushing, receiving, and returning kicks as the Rams outlasted Chicago 41–35. Arnett led the team in rushing in 1958, was third in receiving, and ranked among the league leaders in kickoff and punt returns. He helped the Rams win six of their last eight games to finish 8–4, tied for second with the Bears in the West.

for six home games and drew a record NFL crowd of 102,368 for San Francisco. They averaged 84,000 fans per game in 1958, when they tied for second place in a rare year without a quarterback controversy—Van Brocklin had announced his retirement after the 1957 season, then was traded to Philadelphia. He led the Eagles to the championship two years later.

The Rams had been successful in 1952 when they sent eleven players to the Dallas Texans for linebacker Les Richter, who anchored the defense and went to the Pro Bowl in all of his nine seasons with the club. That was precedent for another blockbuster trade, nine players to the Chicago Cardinals for running back Ollie Matson on February 28, 1959.

Pete Rozelle was the Rams general manager before becoming NFL commissioner.

Pete Rozelle had been the sports information director at the University of San Francisco when the Dons were undefeated in 1951 and sent several players, including Matson, to the NFL. As general manager of the Rams, Rozelle made the trade for Matson, who hopefully was going to be the final piece in the puzzle.

Puzzling was more accurate. Matson was all the player the Rams thought he was, leading the team in rushing in 1959 and, with Arnett, forming part of an explosive kick-return combination. But the players the Rams gave Chicago, while not spectacular, included four starters: defensive tackles Frank Fuller and Art Hauser, defensive end Glenn Holtzman, and offensive tackle Ken Panfil. The Rams also gave up second- and fourth-round draft choices in 1960, plus three 1959 draft picks (Don Brown, Larry Hickman, and John Tracey).

The season came apart after a 2–2 start. The Rams lost eight games in a row. "Put the Lid on Sid," the fans cried. The fifth loss in the streak offered the ultimate indignity. Tied with Philadelphia 20–20 with 1:30 remaining in the game, the Rams were forced to watch Van Brocklin move the Eagles from their 11 yard line to a game-winning field goal with 16 seconds left.

Gillman announced his resignation to the squad before it took the field for the final game against Baltimore in the Coliseum. The coach disclosed after the game that he had been asked to quit. According to the Associated Press, though, the club indicated that it was Gillman's decision.

A new decade was just three weeks away. It would bring monumental changes to the Rams and to pro football.

Reeves and Allen

The Rams closed their disastrous 1962 season on a semihopeful note, taking the defending NFL champion Green Bay Packers into the fourth quarter before losing 20–17, but the game and the 1–12–1 season had little currency amid anticipation of an ownership showdown. The long dispute over who would control operation of the franchise was going to play out in a tense Christmas week sealed-bid auction, winner take all.

On December 27, it was announced that Dan Reeves had outbid his partners Ed Pauley, Hal Seley, and Fred Levy with an offer of $7.1 million, topping the Pauley group's bid by $1 million. Since Reeves already owned one-third of the franchise's shares, he had to purchase his rivals' two-third's shares. His outlay would be $4.8 million for a franchise Reeves bought for $135,000 in 1941.

Under agreement for the auction, held in the presence of NFL commissioner Pete Rozelle, the Pauley group had the opportunity to re-bid at a 20 percent increase—$8.6 million—but declined. The actual cost to Pauley and partners for Reeves's one-third share would have been $2.46 million. The *Los Angeles Times* reported that it was a "surprise victory for the sportsman-broker [Reeves owned a stock brokerage, located next door to the team's Beverly Boulevard offices], bringing to an end a seven-year battle for control of the football team."

By 1964 Reeves's decision to outbid his partners bordered on brilliance. Rozelle had delivered a television contract of $14 million from CBS that guaranteed each team $1 million a year. Television would continue to enrich pro football teams with huge payouts during Rozelle's commissionership, skyrocketing the values of franchises. Not long after winning control of the team, Reeves also sold 49 percent of the Rams to Gene Autry, the singing cowboy and owner of the Los Angeles Angels baseball team, and six others.

After the 1965 season Reeves felt compelled to make a head coaching change. The Rams' overall record since 1959 had been a combined 25–65–4, a .277 winning percentage. Rams attendance had dropped from an average of 83,725 in 1958 to 40,333 in 1965. Seating in the "new look" Coliseum was

George Allen had a 49–19–4
record as Rams coach.

reduced to 72,000 in 1964, but the Rams had only one sellout in the new configuration.

Reeves was determined to get the right head coach and announced on January 10, 1966, that he had appointed George Allen, a forty-three-year-old defensive assistant for the Chicago Bears who had been on Sid Gillman's 1957 Rams staff. Allen was given the job even though several prominent ex-head coaches, including George Wilson, Buddy Parker, and Paul Brown, were mentioned as candidates. University of Southern California coach John McKay had withdrawn his name from consideration.

Allen had joined the Bears in 1958, and his contribution was such that Bears players gave Allen the game ball and serenaded him with a ribald verse on national television after the Bears had beaten the New York Giants 14–10 for the NFL championship in 1963. Chicago's defense forced five turnovers in the game.

The Allen-Reeves relationship would be stormy. From the outset the owner and coach had strong differences on how to build a winner. Reeves believed in the thoroughness of scouting collegiate talent; good use of the waiver system, draft choices, and the signing of free agents; and subjective trading. Allen, whose mantra was "The Future is Now" during his tenure with the Washington Redskins, had little use for draft choices and rookies.

The Rams' 1967 draft echoed the Allen philosophy. They traded their first-, second-, third-, fourth-, fifth-, seventh-, and eighth-round picks. And in 1968 the Rams traded their first-, second-, third-, fourth-, and seventh-round draft choices.

Allen put in long hours, had long practices, and posted slogans all around the Rams practice facility, accentuating commitment and attention to detail. Allen also was a firm

A Matter of Principle

The Rams were stunned when George Halas, the Bears' owner and coach, called the signing of Chicago assistant coach George Allen in 1966 a flagrant case of tampering. "I am shocked that the Los Angeles Rams and their president, Dan Reeves, would attempt to pirate our coaching staff," Halas said. "The Rams were told Allen's legal and binding contract had two years to go and that we expected him to fulfill the terms of his agreement." Insiders and long-time Halas watchers could hardly contain their laughter over this NFL version of the pot calling the kettle black. A founding father of the NFL in 1920, the Bears' curmudgeon had built a great franchise, sometimes with his own definition of the rules.

Few believed Halas would hold Allen to his contract, tradition being not to stand in the way if an assistant coach was offered a head coaching opportunity. But the Bears owner actually took Allen and the Rams to court. Halas spoke so unflatteringly of Allen ("scoundrel" was one adjective) that Vince Lombardi, the legendary coach of the Green Bay Packers, was moved to say to Reeves, "Dan, it looks like you've got a helluva coach!"

After much posturing the Bears owner won the legal test. Old George had a valid contract with the young George. Halas's pompous self-righteousness was surpassed only by his magnanimity. Point made, Halas immediately announced he was freeing Allen to go to the Rams.

Quarterback Roman Gabriel led a
Rams renaissance in the 1960s.
Joe Robbins

believer in a healthy lifestyle. He once told Bob Oates of the *Los Angeles Times* that he believed leisure activity was vital. In Allen's view leisure activity was the "five or six hours at night spent sleeping."

Allen's regimen was tested after the Rams won four of their first five games in 1966. They lost four in a row, including 35–7 at Minnesota and 17–3 to Baltimore at home, but the Rams won their next four, including 21–6 over Minnesota and 21–13 at Baltimore. Trailing Green Bay 27–9 in the fourth quarter of the final game, the Rams had the eventual Super Bowl I–champion Packers perspiring with a comeback that made the final score 27–23. The Rams finished with an 8–6 record, their best since 1958. They were on their way.

Safety Eddie Meador, who played twelve seasons with the Rams, had little to show for his career from 1959 until Allen came on the scene. "I learned more from George Allen than any other coach I played for," said Meador. "He was a great student of the game and he really cared about his players. I don't think he had the same affection for management. I guess George's mistake was bringing in too many veterans. He got results, but sooner or later that catches up to you because eventually you have no draft picks left. I think the front office resented the way he traded so many draft picks."

Allen was known to trade draft choices that he did not possess, resulting in fines from the Commissioner's office. "Everybody believed George ran into problems with management because he shopped off the rookies in favor of veterans," said quarterback Roman Gabriel. "That may have been one reason, but I think another was that he didn't drink or mingle with management. He was more dedicated to the players and winning ball games." Gabriel further noted that Allen's choice of veterans was selective: "He didn't bring in many offensive players. His philosophy was that if you had a good defense you could stay in any game. On offense, he just wanted to keep from turning over the ball."

Early on Allen made his displeasure known with the Rams' in-season practice site, which would not measure up to some high school facilities today. The Rams never trained in opulence, beginning at decrepit Gilmore Stadium near the Beverly Boulevard office. They practiced there until the mid-1950s, at which point the team moved to a recreation park in Burbank, then to another similar site in San Fernando, where the team's dressing room was adjacent to the municipal swimming pool.

By 1967 the Rams had contracted with the City of Long Beach to use Blair Field, a baseball and recreational facility, for $5,000 a year, with the promise to restore the field at the end of each football season. Players, many of whom resided in West Los Angeles or the San Fernando Valley, were moving to more convenient southern Los Angeles County and Orange County communities. Allen lived in nearby Palos Verdes Estates.

The Rams also had bought property and moved their executive offices to an address on West Pico Boulevard in 1964. The distance from the offices to Blair Field was about 30 miles. An us-against-them attitude, which Allen fostered, was easy to develop. It was Allen, his coaches, and players against their opponents, management, ownership, the media, and whomever. It was the coach's way of developing a close-knit team. Almost all of the players bought into the program.

Allen was the first coach to hire an assistant coach dedicated only to special teams, appointing Dick Vermeil in 1969. Allen also made extensive use of the so-called taxi squad of inactive players. "He'd had thirty-five or forty players on the taxi squad," said linebacker Myron Pottios. "When we went out to practice, there would be a hundred guys on the field."

Allen also hired a retired area resident named Ed Boynton to coordinate security. Each morning at daybreak the affable Boynton, nicknamed "007" by the players, would conduct a sweep of Blair Field, religiously opening a deserted baseball press box to see if potential practice spies were hiding. Small drainage holes in the outfield fences were covered with pieces of plywood, although only a snake or gopher would have been able to watch practice from those vantage points. Rams practices were closed to the media, but *Los Angeles Times* reporter Mal Florence found a way to beat the system and the security man. Florence hid in a tree adjacent to the practice field and watched practice one day, then wrote of his experience in the newspaper. There always seemed to be an allegation from the Rams or an opponent about spying. A Rams' assistant is said to have dressed up in a painter's suit with bucket and brush and watched a visiting team work out in the Coliseum before an important game.

The Rams may have been secretive, but they were also becoming successful with Allen who, while trading draft choices, brought in solid and cerebral defensive players who teamed with the dominating front four that included Deacon Jones, Merlin Olsen, Roger Brown, and Lamar Lundy. The breakthrough came in 1967, but the season also portended a future of late-season disappointments for Allen's teams. A 4–0 start was followed by a

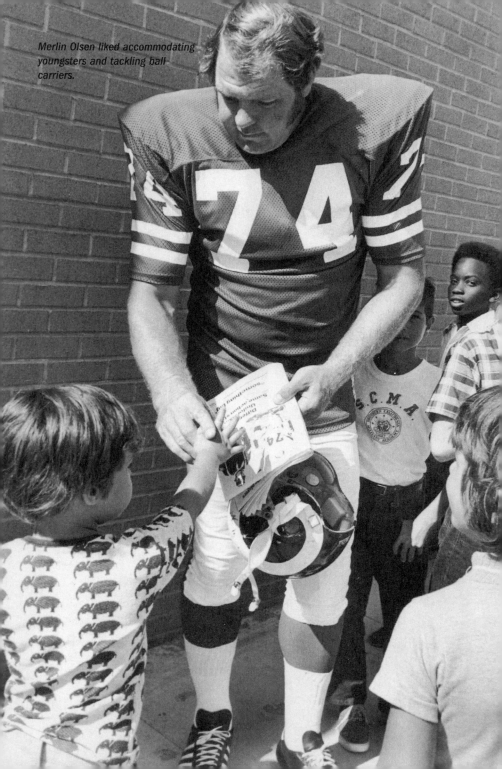

Merlin Olsen liked accommodating youngsters and tackling ball carriers.

pair of ties with San Francisco and Baltimore, then the Rams won out, finishing the regular season with two of the biggest wins in franchise history.

The Rams (9–1–2) were one game behind Baltimore (10–0–2) in the NFL's Coastal Division going into week 13. The Colts played earlier in the day and were in the process of scoring a 30–10 victory over the first-year expansion New Orleans Saints, while the Rams were gearing up against one of the league's toughest teams, the Green Bay Packers, the defending Super Bowl champion.

The Rams defense, blossoming under Allen's guidance, had allowed an average of 8 points in its last five games. Trailing 23–20 in the waning minutes of the game, the Rams blocked a Packers punt, setting up Gabriel's touchdown pass to Bernie Casey for a 27–23 victory. A showdown with Baltimore was next.

A Coliseum crowd of 77,277, the largest for a Rams home game since 1958, turned out on a warm December afternoon to see if Allen's rebuilt team could bring down the mighty Colts, with an 11–0–1 record and future hall of famer Johnny Unitas at quarterback.

It wasn't close. Gabriel completed 18 of 22 passes for 257 yards and 3 touchdowns. One of Gabriel's strikes went to Jack Snow for an 80-yard touchdown. Unitas, who had been trapped for losses thirteen times in the first thirteen games, was hammered into the ground seven times by the Rams' furious defense. The quarterback "sack," so named by its most effective practitioner, Deacon Jones, was becoming a part of the NFL lexicon, although it was not recognized by the league as an official statistic until 1982. The Rams 34–10 victory tied them with

Baltimore, each with 11–1–2 records, but the Rams were declared Coastal Division champions because of a plus-24-points differential in head-to-head meetings.

The most successful regular season in Los Angeles Rams history ended suddenly on a frozen field in Milwaukee the following week. Just two weeks after defeating the Packers, the Rams were beaten 28–7 in the first round of the playoffs. Green Bay thus advanced to its famous "Ice Bowl" game against Dallas and eventually to a Super Bowl II victory over Oakland. Green Bay's Forrest Gregg was almost deified for a performance against the Rams that for years defined the right tackle position. He kept Jones away from Packers quarterback Bart Starr and led a rushing attack that gained 163 yards. Jones, one of the greatest pass rushers in history, never got his footing and was rendered almost immobile on the concretelike Milwaukee Stadium turf.

Allen prepared relentlessly as ever, and the Rams manhandled the Cleveland Browns 30–6 in a meaningless game called the Playoff Bowl, which matched conference runner-ups the week before the Super Bowl.

The Rams made a similar run in 1968, rolling to a 10–1–1 record entering week 13, but they were surprised by the Chicago Bears 17–16 and knocked out of the playoffs by the Colts, losing to Baltimore 28–24 in the final game of the season. A few days later Reeves called Allen. The owner's salutation was, "Merry Christmas, George. You're fired!"

"I had more fun losing with [coach] Svare," Reeves said of his relationship with Allen.

Reaction was swift. Team leaders called a press conference demanding that Allen be reinstated. Gabriel, Jones, Lamar Lundy, Charlie Cowan, Jack Pardee, and Eddie Meador said

All-Pro defensive end Deacon Jones goes through the rope drll.

Winning Ways

George Allen's relationship with management may have been tumultuous, but you can't argue with the results. Allen compiled a record of 49–19–4 over five seasons (1966–70), a winning percentage of .708. Among the twenty coaches in Rams history, only Adam Walsh had a better winning percentage. Walsh went 15–5–1 (.750) over the course of the 1945 and 1946 seasons.

they would retire if Allen was not rehired. When Allen called a press conference to explain his position, twelve players stood behind him. A citizens committee was formed to save Allen's job. Employees in the Rams front office, feeling differently, celebrated Allen's dismissal.

After twelve days of constant media attention, Reeves backed down and agreed to allow Allen back for the final two years of his contract. Speaking of Allen, Reeves said, "If anyone was that dedicated and loved the Rams that much, I should reconsider. He was being a big man about the whole thing."

The Rams were 11–3 in 1969 but beaten at Minnesota 23–20 in the first round of the playoffs on another frozen field. They routed the Cowboys 31–0 in the Playoff Bowl. The Reeves-Allen relationship remained cold to the end. The 1970 season was one in which a late season loss to Detroit effectively knocked the Rams out of the playoffs.

The Rams finished with a 9–4–1 record, and Allen's overall mark of 49–19–4 was the second best ever for a Rams coach. But Allen was released following the season, and Reeves, ailing for some time with Hodgkin's disease, passed away at age fifty-eight on April 15, 1971. Two separate eras for the Rams had ended at virtually the same time.

Days of Rosenbloom

The Rams were in a critical transition in the early 1970s. Dan Reeves was terminally ill with Hodgkin's disease, and George Allen was out for the second time as head coach. In came James Thompson "Tommy" Prothro for the 1971 season. Allen and Prothro were as opposite as Poland and Sri Lanka. Allen traded draft choices for veterans; Prothro traded veterans for draft choices. Prothro had never coached on the professional level; most of Allen's career had been in the pros.

A tall, bluff Southerner and the son of a former Major League Baseball manager, Prothro was a product of military schools and was a Single Wing blocking back for Wallace Wade's Duke Blue Devils, who played Oregon State in the 1942 Rose Bowl. Prothro was Red Sanders's chief assistant at UCLA from 1949 to 1954. The 1954 Bruins were the best in the school's history. They were ranked number one in the country with a Single Wing offense and capped their season by scoring 27 fourth-quarter points to defeat crosstown rival USC 34–0. After this show of force, Prothro was asked to resuscitate an Oregon State program that had posted a 20–36 record in the previous six years.

Prothro took the Beavers to two Rose Bowls and posted an overall record of 63–37–2, then moved to UCLA in 1965 as head coach. The Bruins stunned the collegiate universe by defeating heavily favored USC that year to go to the Rose Bowl, where the Bruins upset undefeated and top-ranked Michigan State. Prothro's record at UCLA was 41–18–3. Including his years at Oregon State, he was 104–55–4 overall. Not as glib as USC's John McKay, Prothro still was glib enough. He was popular and respected in Los Angeles, even though most of the metropolitan media thought McKay was a lock for the Rams job.

The Rams were determined to keep their coaching search a secret. Rams executive Jack Teele registered in a hotel under the name of Jack Russell when he traveled to Memphis, Prothro's hometown, to finalize a five-year contract. Once Prothro signed, Teele returned to his hotel to check out. "But Mr. Russell, your credit card says *Tee-lee*," said the clerk, butchering the pronunciation and sending the Rams official to the parking lot, where Prothro was waiting to take him to the airport. "Tommy, do you have $500 on you?" Teele asked. "Yeah, why?" Prothro responded. Teele explained his problem. Prothro obliged and half-joked, "Are you sure that contract is good?"

The upper end of Prothro's first collegiate draft was outstanding. Linebacker Isiah Robertson was chosen in the first round, defensive end and future hall of famer Jack Youngblood in the second, and safety Dave Elmendorf in the third. All became Pro Bowl players.

Reeves passed away April 15, 1971, and William Barnes was named president and general manager on May 1 by the Rams' nine-person board of directors. Barnes and Mary Reeves, the owner's widow who was named to take Dan's seat on the board, announced that Reeves's 51 percent holdings were not immediately for sale. Barnes was Reeves's longtime friend and business associate whose role would be as a caretaker and to look for a new owner. The asking price would be about $20 million.

On the field veteran Rams players were not taken with Prothro's autocratic manner and his obvious difference from Allen. As a college coach Prothro had dressed in suit, tie, brimmed hat, and dark glasses and carried a briefcase to the field on game days. Most observers believed the luggage contained game plans or special football papers. USC coaching rival John McKay had had a different take. When asked, McKay suggested that Prothro was packing a ham sandwich.

The Rams were 7–4–1 late in Prothro's first season and fighting for a playoff berth when they met the Washington Redskins on a Monday night in Los Angeles. George Allen's

Coke Is It

Rams players in the early 1970s were amazed at some of new coach Tommy Prothro's habits. "Tommy smoked three packs of Camels a day and drank a case, sometimes two cases, of Coke every day," said safety Dave Elmendorf. "That's a lot of Coke and a lot of caffeine. That's a lot of sugar."

Prothro indeed was loyal to Coca-Cola—he had a substantial interest in franchises stretching from northern California into central Oregon.

"Ramskins," as they were called because of the large number of ex-Los Angeles players on the squad, did not let Allen down. Washington sprinted to a 31–10 lead in the third quarter and knocked out the Rams with a fourth-quarter punt return for a touchdown by Leslie "Speedy" Duncan. The 38–24 loss virtually eliminated the Rams from the playoffs, and their final record of 8–5–1 left them a half-game behind San Francisco (9–5) in the 1971 division standings. Allen, on the other hand, led the Redskins to the playoffs with a 9–4–1 record, their best since 1945.

Big changes loomed for the Rams organization. Robert Irsay, a businessman from Skokie, Illinois, and his partner, a former co-owner of the Miami Dolphins, purchased the Rams from Reeves's estate for a reported $19 million in July of 1972. Irsay, who owned a yacht that he christened *The Mighty I*, described himself as "just a tin-knocker [Irsay's term for mechanical contractor] and a happy ex-Marine." His son, James, was a Rams

Rams owner Carroll Rosenbloom displaying a model of Anaheim Stadium.

fan, which played into Irsay's decision. But the principal motive was "money—money's the name of the game," said Irsay.

Speculation already had begun that if the Rams were sold, they would be involved in a history making move. The new owner would trade the franchise to Carroll Rosenbloom in exchange for Rosenbloom's ownership of the Baltimore Colts. Rosenbloom's interest in moving to Los Angeles was not just the Rams. He had become a director for the motion picture giant Warner Brothers and had divested himself of many business interests in the East.

The Rams were regarded as a more expensive property than the Colts, but Rosenbloom said no cash would be exchanged. However, Irsay would receive $1.8 million still due the Colts for their move to the realigned American Football Conference in 1970, plus $200,000 a year for three years for the Rams' continued share of payments for the Colts leaving the NFC for the AFC. (The Colts, Cleveland Browns, and Pittsburgh Steelers each were to be paid $3 million over five years by the ten other NFC teams for agreeing to move to the AFC.) When Rosenbloom and Irsay officially swapped franchises, it was the ownership equivalent of the Rams gaining an all-pro quarterback and the Colts receiving an undrafted rookie offensive lineman.

Rosenbloom was a tough former University of Pennsylvania football player, a friend of the Kennedy family, and a respected old-line NFL owner, having taken over the vagabond Colts franchise in 1953 and turning it into one of the NFL's elite. Until he died tragically in 1979, "C.R." and his wife, Georgia, were at the top of the Los Angeles–Hollywood–Beverly Hills "A" list.

The Rosenbloom-Irsay trade was made official on July 14, 1972, days before the start of training camp. Rosenbloom shook up the Rams front office by immediately installing his Baltimore football executive Don Klosterman as general manager. Prothro was under the gun in 1972. He had traded the popular Rams legend Deacon Jones to San Diego in the off-season ("We did nothing for each other," Jones said of his relationship with Prothro) and had acquired Fred Dryer in a trade with the New York Giants. Only Merlin Olsen remained from the 1960s Fearsome Foursome.

Training camp got off to a bizarre start, with the coach on the cover of *Sports Illustrated*. The magazine published a story in which Karl Sweetan, a former Rams quarterback, was accused of wire fraud and interstate transportation of stolen property. Sweetan was arrested by the FBI after New Orleans Saints coach J. D. Roberts notified the NFL that Sweetan wanted to sell Roberts a Los Angeles Rams playbook.

Indictments never were sought against Sweetan and his cousin because the value of the playbook was estimated at less than what would represent a federal crime. Sweetan, who ended his career with the Rams in 1970, had been a number-one draft choice of the Detroit Lions in 1965. He appeared in the movie *Paper Lion*, and he shared an NFL record after teaming with Pat Studstill on a 99-yard touchdown pass play in 1966.

Deacon Jones weighed in on the controversy. "I can't take it seriously," he said. "I even have an old Rams playbook." Cincinnati coach Paul Brown said, "My goodness. This is an overreaction. Why, I've given some of my retired players playbooks." The game that Sweetan's alleged action would have put in question was the Rams' opener. Los Angeles defeated New Orleans 34–14. It was with this start that the Rams sprinted to a 5–2–1 record, but they lost six of their last seven games.

Prothro was not immediately dismissed at the end of the 6–7–1 season. He had an inconclusive meeting with Rosenbloom in January. Uneasy, Prothro hired an attorney and said to Rosenbloom, "You can tear up the three years on my contract if you want to fire me, but if you fire me in the middle of the season, I'm going to seek all that is coming to me." Rosenbloom's response to Prothro's retaining an attorney was ambivalent. "If that's what you want to do, fine," said the owner. Rosenbloom later said that was when he decided to change coaches.

On January 25, the Rams announced they had signed Chuck Knox to a three-year contract as head coach. Knox had coached professionally as an assistant for ten years with the New York Jets and Detroit Lions. At 2:30 A.M. on January 24 in the living room of Rosenbloom's Bel-Air residence, Knox had looked Rosenbloom in the eye and said, "I can win." Rosenbloom reached over and shook hands with his new coach.

Rosenbloom didn't mention Prothro at Knox's press conference. When asked about Prothro, the owner said Prothro would be paid off but that the two were speaking only through attorneys. Six weeks later, the former coach filed a $1.9 million lawsuit against Rosenbloom, the Rams, and Rosenbloom's former team, the Baltimore Colts. The lawsuit was settled within weeks, after Prothro and Rosenbloom engaged in two or three amicable meetings, but Rosenbloom was not through making changes. The Rams acquired quarterback John Hadl from San Diego and granted quarterback Roman Gabriel his wish by trading him to Philadelphia.

Rosenbloom also made a fashion statement: Gold was returning to the uniform colors. The Rams gold jerseys with blue stripes and numerals had been discarded after a game against Detroit on October 13, 1957, at which point the Rams went to blue jerseys with white trim and white pants with gold trim. Television stations complained that the gold jersey had not presented well when the Rams games were shown to an audience that was mostly watching them on a black-and-white screen. When a suitable gold color was found, owner Dan Reeves refused. Reeves thought there would be fallout because the color was called "buttercup yellow." The Rams went to blue jerseys with white trim and white jerseys with blue trim in 1964. The rest of the uniform was white pants and a white helmet with blue ram horns.

Most of the time, the Rams wore the visiting (white) jerseys at home and on the road, prompting *Los Angeles Herald-Examiner* columnist Bud Furillo to grouse that they resembled a group of ambulance drivers. Don Klosterman, the Rams general manager, took it a step further. "We look like a bunch of vanilla ice-cream salesmen," he said.

Retired Rams equipment manager Don Hewitt remembered that Reeves kept the Rams in white because he wanted fans to be able to see visiting teams in their more colorful home uniforms. Hewitt also was with Rosenbloom on the roof of the Coliseum press box when several uniforms, mixed and matched and designed by David Boss of National Football League Properties, were modeled on the field below. Rosenbloom selected a gold home jersey with ram horns on the shoulders, and an identical white jersey for the road.

The Rams were about to begin the most successful stretch in franchise history, but the playoffs and a perceived lack of offensive pizzazz stalked Knox, despite an overall record of 54–15–1 in the regular season and five consecutive division championships. Knox would wrestle with other problems in this high-profile, high-pressure job. The quarterback controversy, first made famous in Los Angeles two decades before with Bob Waterfield and Norm Van Brocklin, would erupt again.

John Hadl clearly was everyone's choice in 1973. The Rams ran away from the NFC West with a 12–2 record, their best since their championship season in 1945. The two losses were by a combined total of 3 points. They outscored their opponents by more than 200 points.

Hadl, who was named the NFC's player of the year, threw 4 touchdown passes to Harold Jackson in the first half of a game against the Dallas Cowboys. The Rams built a 34–7 lead over the Cowboys, but Dallas battled back and lost just 37–31. That second half was a disturbing precursor to the playoffs several weeks later, when the Cowboys jumped to a 17–0 lead and won the rematch 27–16. Hadl completed only 7 of 23 passes for 133 yards. He was sacked five times, and he had a pass intercepted.

"That was really a great team despite the loss," said running back Lawrence McCutcheon, the Rams top rusher from 1973 to 1977 and still one of the team's all-time leading backs. "It was the best Rams' team that I played on. We had lots of talent, and Chuck brought it together."

James Harris took over as starting quarterback in 1974.

After a 3–2 start and an ignominious 17–6 loss to Green Bay in Milwaukee in 1974, the Rams made a stunning move, trading Hadl to the Packers for five draft choices. James Harris became the quarterback. Harris, one of the first African-Americans to start at quarterback in the NFL, was given the nod over rookie second-round draft choice Ron Jaworski, and he guided the Rams to seven wins in nine games to clinch the NFC West at 10–4. A 19–10 victory over Washington in the divisional playoffs brought the Rams to the doorstep of the Super Bowl.

As circumstance had dictated in the past, the Rams made another pilgrimage to frozen Minneapolis for the NFC Championship Game. Trailing the Vikings 7–3 in the third quarter, Harris marshaled a 98-yard drive that came up scoreless. Harris's 73-yard pass-and-run connection to Harold Jackson put the Rams on Minnesota's 1 yard line. A penalty when guard Tom Mack moved before the snap of the ball set the Rams back, and the Vikings' Wally Hilgenberg intercepted Harris's pass in the end zone on the next play. The teams traded touchdowns in the fourth quarter, and the Vikings won 14–10.

Knox's offense was oriented to power. Harris had a strong passing arm, but Knox wanted to run. The Rams averaged 40 rushes a game and just 24 passes. Rosenbloom chafed. For almost twenty seasons in Baltimore, he had watched Hall of Famer Johnny Unitas pass the Colts to the top of the NFL. The owner wanted flair and excitement. His team was boring and successful.

Harris led the Rams to a 12–2 season in 1975 but was injured, and it was Jaworski who quarterbacked a 35–23, first-round playoff victory over St. Louis. It was the Rams most dynamic postseason performance of the 1970s. Defensive end Jack Youngblood returned an interception 47 yards for a touchdown. Bill Simpson returned another intercepted pass 65 yards for a score. McCutcheon was brilliant, rushing 37 times for 206 yards, both playoff records.

Years later, McCutcheon laughed when he recalled that during the game he looked over to Knox on the sideline. McCutcheon signaled that he wanted to come out for a play to catch his breath. "Chuck pretended he didn't see me—he turned around and went to get a cup of Gatorade," said the player they called "Clutch."

The Rams met the Dallas Cowboys in the NFC Championship Game. Harris's first pass was intercepted, and he was replaced by Jaworski, who was intercepted twice. By the third quarter, Dallas led 34–0. The Cowboys, who made the playoffs as a wild card team, went to Super Bowl X after defeating the Rams 37–7.

The Rams drafted USC quarterback Pat Haden in the seventh round in 1976, further fueling the fire that surrounded the quarterback position. Harris was the preseason starter but broke the thumb on his throwing hand. Jaworski started the regular season opener but was injured, giving way to Haden, who directed a 30–14 victory against Atlanta in his first regular season game.

Haden and Harris, like Van Brocklin and Waterfield twenty-five years before, were a two-headed number-one quarterback. The Rams beat Atlanta 59–0 in the thirteenth game to clinch their fourth straight Western Division title. Haden guided the Rams to their first road playoff win in six tries, 14–12 at Dallas, and the Rams went back to frigid Minnesota for the NFC Championship Game against the Vikings.

Disaster struck early in Minnesota. The Rams drove to the Vikings 1 foot line on their first possession. On fourth down, Knox elected to attempt a field goal. Tom Dempsey's kick was blocked. Minnesota's Bobby Bryant recovered the ball and ran 90 yards for a touchdown. Minnesota went on to win 24–13. It was a sad ending to Merlin Olsen's great Hall of Fame career. In fifteen seasons with the Rams, Olsen earned fourteen Pro Bowl berths. He was the last active member of the original Fearsome Foursome.

More quarterback changes were in the offing in 1977. Jaworski was traded to Philadelphia, and Joe Namath, the New York Jets Super Bowl III legend, was claimed on waivers. Nebraska quarterback Vince Ferragamo, who went to high school in Wilmington, a Los Angeles suburb, was drafted in the fourth round.

Namath could no longer play. After four starts, it was clear that his infirm knees made the future Hall of Famer immobile and ineffective. Haden took over for the last ten games. The Rams were more run-oriented than ever, averaging 44 rushes and 24 passes. McCutcheon pounded for 1,298 yards, John Cappelletti for 598, and Wendell Tyler for 317. The Rams battled to a 10–4 record, going 8–2 down the stretch as they relied on their running game and an outstanding defense that allowed only 146 points. But they were shut out until the last minute of a 14–7 playoff loss to the Vikings.

Questions about Knox's future lingered into January, similar to Prothro's situation previously. Knox had signed a new contract after the 1975 season and had three years to go, but he said he was going to sign a new five-year deal with the Rams. Rams officials, however, confirmed that there were other candidates for the job at that point. Knox eventually left and became the head coach for the Buffalo Bills.

George Allen (with quarterback Pat Haden) returned as coach briefly in 1978.

On February 1, 1978, Rosenbloom hired George Allen as head coach. Yes, that George Allen. The same George Allen who recently had worn out his welcome in Washington. And the same George Allen who had returned the Rams to prominence before falling out with owner Dan Reeves and leaving for the Redskins in 1971.

Best in the West

The Rams set an NFL record when they won seven consecutive NFC Western Division championships from 1973 to 1979. Here's their year-by-year record:

1973   12–2–0   (lost in the first round of the playoffs)

1974   10–4–0   (advanced to the NFC Championship Game)

1975   12–2–0   (advanced to the NFC Championship Game)

1976   10–3–1   (advanced to the NFC Championship Game)

1977   10–4–0   (lost in the first round of the playoffs)

1978   12–4–0   (advanced to the NFC Championship Game)

1979   9–7–0   (advanced to Super Bowl XIV)

It should have been an uneventful preseason. The Rams were routinely favored to win their sixth consecutive division championship and be in the Super Bowl race. But after a 14–7 loss to New England and a 17–0 loss to San Diego, Allen was summarily canned. There was a collective round of sighs and smirks in the Rams front office. Many of the Reeves holdovers had been joined by some of Rosenbloom's newcomers in their dislike of Allen. Rosenbloom stated that Allen had overextended his authority and could not work within the framework prescribed by the owner. Defensive coordinator Ray Malavasi, whose profile had risen with the performance of the Rams defense, was named head coach.

The Rams didn't miss a step. Haden was named NFC player of the year after leading them to a 12–4 record and playoff revenge against Minnesota, 34–10. But if it wasn't Minnesota, it would be the Dallas Cowboys who thwarted the Rams in the NFC Championship Game. After a scoreless first half at the Coliseum, the Cowboys took a 7–0 lead after three quarters, then pulled away to a 28–0 victory. Haden and Ferragamo were intercepted five times.

The events of 1978 went far beyond the playing field. The Rams announced on June 25 that they were moving 25 miles southeast of the Coliseum to the Orange County hub of Anaheim, where they would begin play in 1980 in the enlarged Anaheim Stadium. As early as 1973 Anaheim city fathers had approached Rosenbloom, who was unhappy with the aging Coliseum and who, throughout the 1970s, battled the Coliseum Commission over a number of issues.

The real villain, if there was one, was the Summer Olympic Games. Los Angeles wanted the 1980 games, and that meant the running track, which had been part of the Coliseum facility since its construction, would have to stay in place. Rosenbloom had suggested upgrades to the fifty-year-plus edifice that included lowering the field and putting seats closer to the field (meaning removal of the track); permanent seats in the peristyle end of the field; and better parking, security, media facilities, and fan comforts. Los Angeles did not get the Olympics until 1984, and the track was not removed until years later.

The stadium issue first surfaced on November 19, 1973, when the Rams complained that the Coliseum had not responded to requests for seating improvements and the construction of a nearby practice field. The Coliseum Commission said it wanted the Rams to pay more rent for "what they're getting now," let alone improvements. The occasional bickering went back and forth until March 1978, when Anaheim launched an offensive by taking out a full-page advertisement in the *Los Angeles Times*, urging Rosenbloom to move the franchise to Anaheim Stadium, "a modern, attractive place to watch professional football."

Coliseum Commission honcho Kenneth Hahn indignantly portrayed the advertisement as "a declaration of war between officials of Los Angeles County and Orange County and [it] would be met head-on." Hahn added, "We are not going to let the Los Angeles Rams become the Orange Rams."

On April 2, a *Los Angeles Times* editorial-page writer preached temperance, patience, and negotiation and criticized Hahn's saber rattling: "After all, Los Angeles took the Dodgers from Brooklyn, the Lakers from Minneapolis, and, yes, the Rams from Cleveland." Then, after Rich Roberts's *Los Angeles Times* report on April 28 that "Carroll Rosenbloom is going to move his Rams to Orange County, lock, stock, and shoulder pads," Hahn claimed Anaheim city officials were "bluffing," but admitted that Rosenbloom had told him, "Anaheim gave me an offer I couldn't refuse."

The move became official July 25, 1978. The Los Angeles Rams would begin playing in a 69,000-seat Anaheim Stadium in 1980. The cost to increase seating in the 43,000-plus baseball park would be about $22 million. Rosenbloom also would be personally involved in a $125 million commercial development on ninety-five acres surrounding the stadium. The Rams were moving their in-season training facility and practice fields to a redesigned elementary school location 3 miles from the stadium in West Anaheim in time for the 1979 season.

Rosenbloom was asked if he would object to a team moving into Los Angeles to replace the Rams as Coliseum tenants. "If my twenty-seven partners [the other NFL owners] decide they want to put another team in California—or if they want to put one in Hong Kong—I could not vote against that," he replied. Rosenbloom did not know, nor would he live to see, the battle for Los Angeles and the Coliseum. The Oakland Raiders would move there in 1982 after a protracted court fight with the NFL.

The Magic Kingdom

On April 2, 1979, Carroll Rosenbloom, the seventy-two-year-old owner of the Los Angeles Rams, went for a swim near his winter oceanfront home in Golden Beach, Florida, north of Miami. There was heavy surf in the Atlantic Ocean. Rosenbloom, who had undergone heart surgery two years before, was an experienced ocean swimmer but was pulled out to sea by a strong undertow. A Canadian tourist walking on the beach heard Rosenbloom cry for help. According to news reports, Rosenbloom was dead by the time rescuers reached him. The local coroner said an autopsy confirmed that the owner had drowned. "The waves were extremely rough," said Golden Beach police chief William Henrikson. "We were dragged almost 150 yards north along the beach during the rescue try."

Rosenbloom's death cast a pall over the Rams organization and was felt throughout the NFL. He was remembered as a strong, vocal owner who was committed to winning. He had accomplished that with two franchises, Baltimore and Los Angeles. Rosenbloom's teams posted a regular-season record of 232–122–8, a .652 winning percentage. The Colts and Rams won a combined eleven division or conference championships and three NFL titles. Their playoff record was 12–10. It was a remarkable football legacy.

The owner's son, Steve, who had worked in the Colts and Rams organizations since he was a teenager, was the presumptive heir to Rosenbloom's position, but the owner's widow, Georgia, was first in the line of succession according to Rosenbloom's will. Georgia fired Steve, who was her stepson, not long after assuming control of the organization and retained Don Klosterman as general manager.

With this backdrop the Rams forged ahead in 1979, favored to win their seventh consecutive division championship. In a most unlikely season, the Rams were one game under .500 at 5–6 after the eleventh week. They were reeling from a succession of injuries to starters John Cappelletti, Ron Jessie, and a score of other players, plus the retirement of guard Tom Mack, a future member of the Pro Football Hall of Fame. Battle tested, the

Georgia Frontiere has been the
Rams boss since 1979.

Rams won four of their last five games to finish 9–7, first in the West. Only the 1963 Boston Patriots (7–6–1) and the 1978 Minnesota Vikings (8–7–1) had won division championships with poorer records.

Even more unlikely the Rams, who were beaten 30–6 by Dallas and 40–16 by San Diego on successive weeks during a three-game losing streak in the regular season, defeated Dallas 21–19 and Tampa Bay 9–0 in the playoffs to earn a berth in Super Bowl XIV against the Pittsburgh Steelers.

The Super Bowl was played in January of 1980 at the Rose Bowl in Pasadena, California, before a record crowd of more than 103,000. It marked the first time a team had played in the Super Bowl in its home market. For a while it appeared the Rams might conclude their miracle season with a victory over the favored Steelers. Pittsburgh quarterback Terry Bradshaw, however, forged a 17-point fourth quarter that brought the Steelers from behind for a 31–19 victory. Los Angeles soon was in the Rams rearview mirror. Anaheim, Disneyland's Magic Kingdom, and thirty other Orange County communities awaited the franchise's arrival in time for the 1980 season.

Anaheim sure was different from Los Angeles. The Rams executive offices and in-season training headquarters were located on the campus of Juliette Low Elementary School, which had been closed and reconfigured for the team's arrival. The move by the Rams to this type of facility started a trend in the NFL. Others followed suit, including the Oakland Raiders, who headquartered at an El Segundo junior high when they moved to Los Angeles in 1982.

Juliette Low, renamed Rams Park, was located on Lincoln Avenue in West Anaheim. It offered a mostly quiet, relaxed atmosphere in a very diverse environment. To the north of the park, hidden from the practice field by a huge stand of euca- lyptus trees and a tarp covering a cyclone fence, was the Dad Miller municipal golf course. Tiger Woods, who attended nearby Western High in the early 1990s, played many rounds as a junior golfer on that course. To the east of the facility was a quiet resi- dential street lined with stucco houses and neatly manicured lawns. To the south was a driveway and parking for a two-story office building fronting Lincoln Avenue. The Rams entry and parking lot did not face the busy thoroughfare. To the west, on Lincoln, was an apartment complex, coffee shop, and a motel in which the Rams temporarily housed newly arrived coaches or scouts and other personnel.

A few scouts and assistant coaches were startled—and slightly embarrassed—one morning when they witnessed the Anaheim Police Department vice squad completing a sting operation by arresting several women in the hotel lobby. The women were charged with practicing what generally has been described as the world's oldest profession. Coaches and scouts were humorously and aggressively quizzed by their associates on whether they had participated in any of the alleged activity. Todd Hewitt, who succeeded his father, Don Hewitt, as equipment manager, occa- sionally was propositioned upon arriving for work in the morning.

There also were frequent visits by vagrants and panhandlers, to the point that the Rams established a manned security post at the front of the facility. This did not keep one homeless person from constructing a shelter in the far northeast reach of the orig- inal playground. He was discovered after a short time. A worker on the facility landscape crew was found to have been sleeping in a car in the parking lot for several weeks. After being dismissed, he later was discovered snoring blissfully in the parking lot Dumpster.

"After Blair Field, we thought the grammar school was the Taj Mahal," said Hewitt, "but as we moved along to the late 1980s and early 1990s, it gradually became outmoded. It was not in the best area, and it was too small."

The Rams made a splash in Orange County, averaging 62,531 fans for eight home games at Anaheim Stadium in 1980. They scored 424 points, their most since 1950, and gained more than 6,000 yards. Vince Ferragamo, having wrested the starting job from Pat Haden at quarterback, passed for 30 touchdowns, but the division championship eluded the Rams for the first time since 1973. The Rams' 11–5 record was second to Atlanta's 12–4, although late-season victories of 38–14 over Dallas and 20–17 over the Falcons gave rise to playoff hopes. Los Angeles made it in as a wild card team, but history would not be rewritten. Dallas ended the Rams' season for the fourth time in six years with a victory in the opening round of the playoffs. The Cowboys pushed the Rams around with 338 yards rushing and outscored them 21–0 in the second half of a 34–13 win.

The clock began to wind down on head coach Ray Malavasi's tenure, beginning with player retirement, defection, and offseason trades. The 1981 season was diminished before the first snap of the ball. Linebacker Bob Brudzinski retired. Ferragamo, embroiled in a contract dispute, bolted to Montreal of the Canadian Football League, and linebacker Jack "Hacksaw" Reynolds was traded to San Francisco.

Pat Haden was the starting quarterback again, with Jeff Rutledge as backup. Defensive end Fred Dryer, who had played in 174 consecutive games, was benched for the first time in his fourteen-season career. Dryer had been cut in training camp but returned to the squad. He did not play in the opening game, although fans cheered him in support as he sat on the bench. Center Rich Saul retired at the end of the 6–10 season after playing in 176 consecutive games.

Ferragamo returned from Canada in 1982, but the Rams traded for Baltimore quarterback Bert Jones. After leading the Rams to a 23–0 halftime lead in the opening game at Green Bay, Jones and his teammates were stunned by a second-half come-back that resulted in a 35–23 Packers victory. Following the Rams' 0–2 start that season, play was suspended by a sixty-day NFL players' strike. The Rams never recovered, finishing with a 2–7 record, including a 37–31 loss to the former Oakland Raiders, who had moved into the Los Angeles Coliseum. Malavasi, 8–17 in his final twenty-five games, was fired.

A new era was heralded on February 14, 1983, when former college coach John Robinson was named head coach. Robinson had posted a 67–14–1 record in seven seasons after replacing John McKay at USC in 1976.

Robinson had turned down an offer to coach the New England Patriots after the 1981 season and had resigned from the USC coaching position just three months before coming to the Rams. He had been working as a vice president at the university. "I thought I wanted to be out of football, but it's in my blood," said Robinson, whose USC teams overpowered opponents with their offensive version of "Student Body Right" and "Student Body Left."

Robinson quickly moved to bring this brand of football to the Rams. After the Baltimore Colts selected Stanford quarterback John Elway with the first choice in the 1983 draft (he was even-

The Rams' Eric Dickerson set NFL rushing records in the 1980s.

tually traded to the Denver Broncos), the Rams took Southern Methodist running back Eric Dickerson with the second pick. Dickerson, fast, strong, and 6'3" and 220 pounds, was perfect for the new Rams coach's one-back offense.

Robinson gave the football to Dickerson. Begoggled and with a majestic running style, Dickerson took the NFL by storm. He set league rookie records with 390 carries, 1,808 yards rushing, and 18 touchdowns. Dickerson won NFL player of the year honors, and Robinson was the league's coach of the year. The Rams recovered from two poor seasons with a 9–7 record. A 24–17 win over Dallas in the wild card game sparked hopes of a deep run in the playoffs, but the victory was followed by a 51–7 blowout loss to Washington.

Dickerson rushed for more than 100 yards in twelve games in 1984 and set an NFL record with 2,105 yards rushing, but the Rams lost the wild card game to the New York Giants 16–13. That year Jeff Kemp (the son of U.S. Congressman Jack Kemp, the former pro football quarterback) replaced Ferragamo as the starting quarterback. In turn Kemp would be succeeded by Dieter Brock in 1985.

There were two unmistakable trends surrounding the 1980s Rams. They annually were searching for the quarterback who could lead them to the Super Bowl, and key veteran players were involved in contract disputes, some of epic proportion. Dickerson became disenchanted and held out for the first two games of the 1985 season. His contract renegotiated, Dickerson returned to lead the Rams to an 11–5 record and the NFC West championship.

Dallas and Los Angeles met in the playoffs for the eighth time in thirteen seasons. Dickerson rushed 34 times for 248 yards and

Record Run

Eric Dickerson set an NFL record when he rushed for 2,105 yards in 1984. Here's a game-by-game look at his historic season:

OPPONENT	ATTEMPTS	YARDS	AVERAGE	TOUCHDOWNS
Dallas	21	138	6.6	1
Cleveland	27	102	3.8	0
at Pittsburgh	23	49	2.1	0
at Cincinnati	22	89	4.0	1
N.Y. Giants	22	120	5.0	0
Atlanta	19	107	5.6	2
at New Orleans	21	164	7.8	0
at Atlanta	24	145	6.0	1
San Francisco	13	38	2.9	0
at St. Louis	21	208	9.9	0
Chicago	28	149	5.3	2
at Green Bay	25	132	5.3	0
at Tampa Bay	28	191	6.8	3
New Orleans	32	160	5.0	1
Houston	27	215	8.0	2
at San Francisco	26	98	3.8	1
Totals	379	2,105	5.6	14

scored on runs of 55 and 40 yards. The Rams 20–0 victory sent them into the NFC Championship Game against the Bears in Chicago. But on a freezing Midwestern afternoon, the Rams were beaten 24–0 by the Bears, who went on to a 46–10 victory over the New England Patriots in Super Bowl XX.

Dickerson's contract problems created the most news for the team in 1985, but a more compelling event took place early in training camp. Defensive end Jack Youngblood retired after fourteen seasons. Youngblood was a warrior in the true sense of the word, a "spit-on-it-and-tape-it-up" player who ignored injuries. He played in 201 consecutive games and 202 overall. With Fred Dryer, Larry Brooks, and Cody Jones, Youngblood formed the second incarnation of the Rams' "Fearsome Foursome" defensive line, first made famous by Deacon Jones, Merlin Olsen, Lamar Lundy, and Rosey Grier.

Jones was the most famous practitioner of the quarterback sack before the NFL recognized the statistic in 1982. Youngblood was not far behind, but the tall, handsome native of Monticello, Florida, also was remembered for his inspirational persona and the ability to make the big play. His effort against the St. Louis Cardinals in the 1975 playoffs was memorable. On one play Youngblood knocked future Hall of Fame tackle Dan Dierdorf off the line into the Cardinals backfield; tipped and intercepted Jim Hart's pass; and raced 47 yards for the Rams' first touchdown in a 35–23 victory.

Many still remember the broken left fibula that Youngblood incurred in the 1979 playoffs against Dallas, after his foot caught on the Texas Stadium Astroturf and he collided with Cowboys tackle Rayfield Wright. X-rays taken at halftime confirmed the broken leg. Youngblood advised team doctor Clarence Shields to "tape it up." "I can't tape up a broken leg," said Shields. "What's there to tape? It's broken."

"We ended up strapping the leg," Youngblood recalled. "And I played the second half. I even chased Roger Staubach out of bounds and got a sack."

Youngblood started and played the next two games as the Rams went to Super Bowl XIV. His legendary toughness had carried him through other major injuries during his career. Finally, seventeen years after retirement, Youngblood was named to the Pro Football Hall of Fame in 2001, along with teammate Jackie Slater. It was a belated honor for a man who had given so much to his team and who had played so well against the best offensive tackles in the game.

Slater, a tackle from Jackson State in Mississippi, was a third-round draft choice of the Rams in 1976 and played twenty seasons with the club before retiring in 1995. Slater and Dennis Harrah were the point men for Robinson's power running game, which reached a peak in 1986.

Still looking for a quarterback, the Rams started the 1986 season with Steve Dils and Steve Bartkowski but traded for Houston's Jim Everett four weeks into the season. Everett, who seemed destined for a great career, represented the first of two blockbuster trades the Rams would make in 1986 and 1987. With uncertainty at quarterback (Dils and Bartkowski split time until Everett took over for the final five games), the Rams went to Dickerson. He averaged more than 25 rushing attempts a game and had 404 for the season, three attempts short of the NFL record.

Dickerson was in the lineup and was once again an unhappy player when there was another players' strike after the second game of the 1987 season, with the Rams at 0–2. This time the

Defensive end Jack Youngblood was a classic NFL warrior.

NFL suspended play just one week, then used replacement players until the veterans came back to work three games later. By that time the Rams were 1–4 with a Monday night game coming up at Cleveland. Dickerson scored an early touchdown but aggravated an injury and watched the second half from the sideline as a national television audience wondered what was going on.

"John [Robinson] knows I'm not a faker," Dickerson said later. "I never faked, and my leg was bothering me at the time. It tightened up on that [touchdown] run. When I went in [at half-time], it was really sore and John said, 'Don't play. Don't go back in. We don't want to take the risk of your getting hurt.'"

At the end of his conversation with Rich Roberts of the *Los Angeles Times*, however, Dickerson was more expansive: "I know I've never been hurt. I probably could have played. If it had been a serious, serious situation I probably could have played. But I felt like I had given them so much . . . and they just weren't thankful for it."

After the 30–17 loss to Cleveland, a league meeting was held in Kansas City. Indianapolis general manager Jim Irsay approached Rams vice president John Shaw. "We talked very casually," said Irsay. "The feeling around the league was that they weren't going to trade [Dickerson]." The first indication that something was up, however, came four days before a game with division rival San Francisco. The Rams deactivated Dickerson, declaring that he was "physically and mentally unable to play."

On Saturday the Rams traded Dickerson to the Colts after discussions that also included Buffalo, St. Louis, Houston, and Minnesota. "I felt I could no longer play for the Rams," said Dickerson. "Management felt like I had turned on them. I felt they turned on me. John Shaw did not lie. He also said I was the best player they had . . . had ever had, but he wasn't willing to pay."

The Rams began to regroup. Robinson went to one of his favorite players, Charles White, to replace Dickerson. White had won the Heisman Trophy as Robinson's USC tailback in 1979, and he responded with a 1,374-yard season and 11 touchdowns. After a disastrous 1–7 start, the Rams won five games in a row and finished 6–9. Dave Anderson, the *New York Times'* Pulitzer prize–winning columnist, declared the Dickerson trade "the biggest in NFL history," as far as a possible shift of power in the AFC and for what amounted to eight players for the Rams (six future draft choices and two current running backs).

But monster trades were nothing new to the Rams. They sent eleven players to the Dallas Texans for linebacker Les Richter in 1953. They traded eight players and a draft choice to the Chicago Cardinals for running back Ollie Matson in 1959. In 1971 the Rams sent six players, including veteran stars Jack Pardee and Maxie Baughan, to the Washington Redskins for tight end Marlin McKeever and seven draft choices. In 1986 the Rams obtained Jim Everett from Houston for two first-round draft choices, a fifth-round draft choice, and two players.

Everett blossomed into one of the league's top quarterbacks, passing for 31 touchdowns and almost 4,000 yards in 1988. Henry Ellard caught 86 passes for 1,414 yards that year, and Greg Bell was a 1,212-yard rusher, having replaced White. A late season upset loss to San Diego deprived the Rams of a division championship, but they earned a wild card playoff berth (Los Angeles was eliminated by Minnesota in the first round).

As the decade drew to a close, the Rams could point to seven playoff appearances and an overall record of 86–66 in Orange

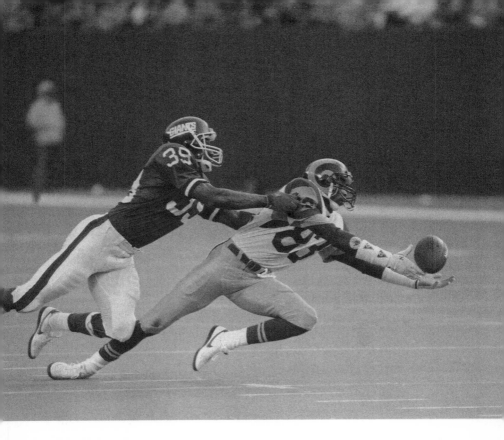

Flipper Anderson scored the winning touchdown in the 1989 playoff game against the New York Giants.

County. They were 78–50, not including the two strike seasons. Average attendance in 1989 was still good (58,846), but down a few thousand from the first year in Orange County. The trend would continue.

The last season of the 1980s represented one of the Rams' greatest accomplishments and one of their most bitter disappointments. They were 11–5 for the third time since moving, but the Rams again finished behind San Francisco, which had taken control of the NFC West and would win four Super Bowls in the decade. The Rams took their playoff hopes on the road, in the cold East, in the wild card round. With Bell pounding away for 124 yards and Everett passing for 281, the Rams opened with a solid 21–7 win at Philadelphia, advancing to the divisional playoff round and another trip east to New York.

In a gritty battle with the favored Giants, the Rams won 19–13 in overtime, and the vision of wide receiver Willie "Flipper" Anderson scoring the winning touchdown remains on often seen NFL Films highlight reels today. Anderson took Everett's 30-yard pass with 1:06 gone in overtime and never stopped running—out of the end zone, through the tunnel of the players entrance, and into the Rams' winning locker room.

The victory set up the NFC Championship Game against the 49ers in San Francisco. Los Angeles had won there 13–12 early in the year and lost to the 49ers 30–27 in Anaheim late in the season. The Rams were 5–4 in regular season games in San Francisco from 1980 to 1989, and they had a good feeling about themselves and the game.

It never was close. The Rams did not score after Mike Lansford's 23-yard field goal to give them a 3–0 lead in the first quarter. Three second-quarter touchdowns gave the 49ers a 21–3 lead at halftime. They outgained the Rams 442 yards to 156 and won 30–3. Everett came under criticism when he ducked and went down on a phantom quarterback sack late in the game. Everett felt pressure when there was none; some cynics said that "he sacked himself."

Everett's career and the Rams' fortunes took a downturn after that. Neither would be the same in the 1990s.

The Kurt Warner Saga

Boyhood dreams. A never-ending passion for the game. Older than any rookie. He came out of nowhere to become a legendary player . . . with almost divine talent. That was Roy Hobbs, as played by Robert Redford in the classic 1984 baseball motion picture *The Natural*. That, too, was Kurt Warner, the quarterback whose long journey to the National Football League's center stage in 1999 was the stuff of story books and fairy tales.

Seldom a starter in college, Warner was not drafted out of the University of Northern Iowa and was a rookie free agent, the fourth quarterback in the Green Bay Packers training camp in 1994, buried on the depth chart behind Brett Favre, Mark Brunell, and Ty Detmer. Released before the season by the Packers, Warner could not hook on with another NFL team. He went back to Iowa to his home in Cedar Rapids and took a job in a HyVee grocery store, stocking shelves for $5.50 an hour. Unable to catch on with a team in the NFL's Europe League the following spring, Warner signed with the Iowa Barnstormers of the Arena League.

He thrived on the small field. The Arena game, played eight men to a side on a 50-yard grid, is about half the width of an NFL field. Passing represents about 90 percent of the plays. Warner threw for 183 touchdowns in three seasons, including 79 in one year. The Arena League was not the big field of the NFL, but Warner plugged away with the Barnstormers. The money wasn't great. With incentives, the 6'2", 215-pounder made as much as $65,000 a year but supplemented his income in the off-season with various jobs. Warner needed the extra money because he had taken on an additional responsibility, one born of love and faith.

Kurt was in college when he and a Northern Iowa teammate went to a country music dance club in Cedar Falls in 1992. There Kurt met Brenda Meoni, a single mother living with her parents and on food stamps. Brenda's mother had talked her daughter into going out that night, just to get Brenda's thoughts on something other than the heartache that visited her daily. One of Brenda's children, son Zachary, was blinded and sustained brain damage when he was accidentally dropped to the floor by Brenda's husband. The guilt and unhappiness that followed led to their divorce.

Though taken with the modest, darkly handsome younger man she met on the dance floor that night, Brenda was realistic. At the end of the evening, she explained to Warner that she had two children and would understand if he didn't want to see her again.

But Warner was smitten. He coaxed her address and showed up the next morning, a rose in hand and wanting to meet the kids. Brenda explained how her former husband had taken the four-month-old Zachary out of the bathtub, and the baby slipped from his father's hands and hit the back of his head on the side of the tub. "Initially they told Brenda that Zachary would be lucky to live," recalled Warner. "They said he probably never would sit up and definitely would not walk." Zachary overcame some long odds. He walks and talks like any other youngster. He has required special assistance with schoolwork, but he can see things when they are close to his face.

Warner faced some long odds himself in another realm. The Arena League was fine, but he wanted the NFL, which was not particularly interested in him. Rams personnel chief Charlie Armey, who knew Warner's college coach, finally arranged for Kurt to try out with the Rams on November 25, 1997. The NFL season was coming to a close, and the Rams, under first-year coach Dick Vermeil, were headed to a 5–11 season with Tony Banks at quarterback. "Dick and I and Jerry Rhome, our quarterbacks coach, worked out Warner," said Armey. "Vermeil liked him."

Warner, however, thought the tryout was so bad that he didn't think the Rams would show any additional interest.

Kurt Warner led the Rams to a Super Bowl XXXIV victory over the Tennessee Titans.

Recently married, Warner and Brenda headed to Jamaica for their honeymoon, with a scheduled workout with the Chicago Bears coming after that. During the honeymoon, Warner was bitten on his right elbow, possibly by a scorpion or a centipede. He was on antibiotics for almost a month and never worked out for the Bears.

The Rams, however, made a move. On December 26, 1997, six days after the end of the season, the Rams signed Warner to a 1998 contract. He was allocated to the Amsterdam Admirals of NFL Europe, coached by Al Luginbill, a former American college coach who was looking for a quarterback and had mentioned Warner to the Rams after watching Kurt in an Arena League game.

Warner adopted Zachary and his sister, Jesse, before he went to Europe. It was a beautiful moment for all, especially Brenda, who had endured more tragedy in 1996. Her parents were killed when a tornado swept through their retirement home in Arkansas.

Warner led NFL Europe in yards passing, attempts, completions, and touchdown passes. He made the Rams as their number-three quarterback in training camp in 1998. Rhome liked the left-handed Will Furrer for number three, but Vermeil chose Warner. Furrer's fate may have been determined at the end of the final preseason game in Dallas. He spiked the ball to stop the clock, although time had run out, and the game was over.

The Rams staggered to a 4–12 record behind quarterbacks Banks and Steve Bono in 1998. Banks, a second-round draft choice in 1996, was smart, had a strong arm, and was athletic, but he wore out his welcome with erratic play and acts of immaturity. Banks infuriated the coaching staff when he didn't accompany the team home after a 14–0 loss at Miami midway through the season.

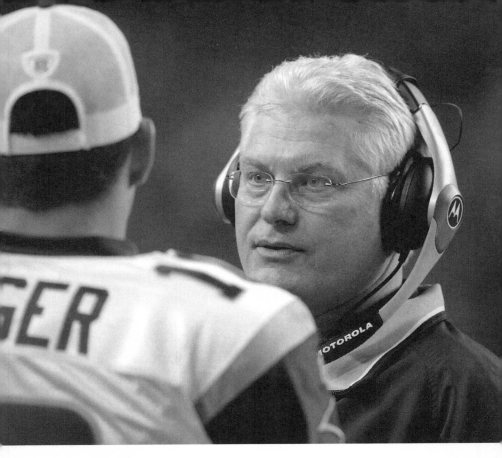

Rams coach Mike Martz's offense became known as "The Greatest Show on Turf."

The final game of the year was a 38–19 blowout loss at San Francisco. Warner, who did not play for fifteen straight games, was active for the first time in the fourth quarter. Mopping up he completed 4 of 11 passes for 39 yards. Vermeil conducted a player personnel meeting with his staff following the final game. The subject of Banks was on the table. Vermeil had not made up his mind, but offensive line coach Jim Hanifan, a twenty-five-season NFL veteran, spoke up. "If he's our quarterback next year, put your houses up for sale," Hanifan advised his colleagues. "We'll all be fired."

The Rams signed free agent Trent Green from the Washington Redskins and traded Banks to Baltimore. Green had led the Redskins to a 6–3 record after seven straight losses to open the 1998 season and was going to be reunited in St. Louis with Mike Martz, who was hired from Washington to be the Rams offensive coordinator. Green had attended Vianney High in South St. Louis before going to Purdue. A seventh-round draft choice who was cut by San Diego, Green blossomed in Washington. He was coming home not as a conquering hero but as a vision of hope for the downtrodden Rams, who weeks later would trade with Indianapolis for running back Marshall Faulk.

Warner may have wondered where he fit, although the departure of Banks had elevated Kurt to the backup role as number two. Green was outstanding in the preseason, completing 28 of 32 passes, but he went down with a season-ending knee injury in the third preseason game against San Diego. Green's injury cast a pall over Rams Park. Some on the coaching staff wanted Vermeil to sign the talented but enigmatic Jeff George. Others suggested the veteran Jeff Hostetler, who had retired after the 1997 season.

Vermeil wasn't swayed. His voice breaking with emotion, Vermeil addressed his weekly day-after-the-game news conference: "We will rally behind Kurt Warner and play good football."

Warner's first start was in Detroit in the final preseason game. He led the Rams to a field goal on the first series and directed a 17–6 victory. The game marked the beginning of one of the most remarkable runs in NFL history, leading to two Super Bowl appearances in three seasons and a possible Hall of Fame future.

But injuries and other factors, some impossible to control, led to Warner's exit from St. Louis in 2004.

Warner signed with the New York Giants and led them to a 5–2 start. After successive losses to Chicago and Arizona, Warner was replaced by Eli Manning, the first selection in the 2004 NFL draft. The Giants did not win again, finishing with a 5–11 record.

Warner announced at the end of the season that he was not going to return to the Giants in 2005. "I loved my year here, but I'm not content in being a backup," said Warner. "I think I showed people and won games and have proven I can play and start in this league." Warner apparently met criteria in his two-year contract with the Giants that allowed him to void the final year and become a free agent. He would sign with the Arizona Cardinals and try to recover the magic of those magical years in St. Louis.

Kurt Warner in St. Louis

Kurt Warner enjoyed a remarkable run in St. Louis. In 1999 he joined Roman Gabriel as the only Rams players to earn the Associated Press's NFL Most Valuable Player award. (Running back Marshall Faulk has since also joined the group.) That year Warner became just the second player in league history to pass for 40 touchdowns in a season (he had 41). Two years later Warner was named the MVP again after throwing for 4,830 yards—at the time the second highest single-season total in NFL history—and compiling a passer rating of more than 100 for the second time (101.4). Here are Warner's statistics in his six years with the Rams:

YEAR	GAMES	ATT	COMP	PCT	YDS	TD	INT	RATING
1998	1	11	4	36.4	39	0	0	47.2
1999	16	499	325	65.1	4,353	41	13	109.2
2000	11	347	235	67.7	3,429	21	18	98.3
2001	16	546	375	68.7	4,830	36	22	101.4
2002	7	220	144	65.5	1,431	3	11	67.4
2003	2	65	38	58.5	365	1	1	72.9
Totals	53	1,688	1,121	66.4	14,447	102	65	97.2

The Road to the Super Bowl

Great accomplishments almost always are accompanied by a moment that by itself may seem meaningless. For the 1999 St. Louis Rams, who defeated the Tennessee Titans 23–16 in Super Bowl XXXIV, that moment happened for me after the third game of the season, while waiting for the arrival of the team's charter airplane at the Cincinnati airport in Covington, Kentucky. Whether it was a group of Rams players and coaches lounging in the airport restaurant watching the Sunday night game on ESPN or others chilling out and grooving with electronic listening devices, I noticed that they all began to demonstrate a common body language. The Rams had a swagger. They'd also come together as a team. They were 3–0 and knew they were good—and their opponents knew they were good.

The Rams also had avoided some unwanted team history that day. Their 38–10 victory over the Cincinnati Bengals, in what had been described as the "Lousy Bowl," all but assured the Rams that they would not be the first team to lose one hundred games in the decade of the 1990s. They were 47–99 going into the game; Cincinnati was 48–98.

It had been almost ten years since a 30–3 loss to San Francisco in the NFC Championship Game, a game that took on more significance with each passing season. The 1989 defeat by the 49ers overshadowed the Rams' run through the playoffs from the wild card position, their 6–1 record down the stretch in the regular season, and a year of battling back from adversity.

The Rams' 11–5 regular season record in 1989 was punctuated by Flipper Anderson's setting an NFL record with 336 yards receiving on 15 catches in a 20–17 overtime win against division contender New Orleans. Jackie Slater was named the NFC offensive lineman of the year for the third straight season and the fifth time in his career. Jim Everett threw for 29 touchdowns, and Greg Bell was the fourth different Rams player to rush for at least 1,000 yards in a decade in which Rams' leading rushers went over 1,200 yards six times.

The 1989 Rams not only made two successful cross-country trips in the playoffs, they also had clinched the wild card berth in the final week of the regular season after another cross-country jaunt to New England, where they hung on for a 24–20 victory over the Patriots. The Rams traveled more than 15,000 miles on three weekends. Perhaps because of what they had overcome, the loss to the 49ers was more devastating. That group of Rams never recovered from the defeat, and quarterback Jim Everett struggled to come to terms with the "phantom sack" that took place late in the third quarter with the 49ers leading 24–3.

Everett gave the appearance of giving up at one point. Back to pass in the pocket, he suddenly went to the ground, brought his knees to chest, and covered the football. San Francisco pass rushers had surrounded Everett, but none touched him.

"Everett felt the bullet when there were no bullets," said CBS television game analyst John Madden. "I don't know if I've ever seen a quarterback get knocked down when there was no contact. In this game you've got to keep that head up and keep working to finding an opening. You should not feel a guy behind you."

Everett was oblique after the game when asked about the play. "I was trying to look upfield, and I think they rushed three guys," he said. "They had everybody covered, and I tried to step up and throw. Then in the corner of my eye, I saw someone coming and I thought he was going to take a shot. I ducked under it." Pressed, Everett continued: "I thought the guy was going right at me, and I tried to duck. Someone's barreling in on you and it's a split-second decision. I was just trying to get the hell out of the way."

Always image conscious and with a politician's flair for verbiage, Everett appeared perplexed by the questioning. "I don't think it's going to make any highlight films, is it?" he said nervously. The quarterback's explanation was accepted neither by the media nor, in turn, by the fans. The issue never was settled. Everett felt he should have been judged as the Rams' all-time passing leader and not by one play. "I've got the heart of a lion," he once said. "I think my courage is impeccable. I stand in there as good as anybody . . . ."

Everett went into the 1990 season with a new, six-year contract worth a reported $2.2 million a year. He bypassed free agency and said, "I look at baseball players, and I think kids out there get the impression they play more for the money than the sport. I wanted to be a Ram. I don't think more money would make Jim Everett happy. The fact is, I want to be here."

On the surface all seemed well. But the Rams fell to 5–11 in 1990. Coach John Robinson fired coordinator Fritz Shurmur and five other defensive coaches after the season. "We're going to change our approach on defense," Robinson explained. "I want to go to a more aggressive, attacking type of philosophy. We've been a defense that's been deteriorating, and it was just a question of what I felt was the solution to get us going again."

It was a cosmetic move. The Rams bottomed out with a 3–13 record in 1991. Everett's 1990 and 1991 statistics included 60 sacks, 34 touchdown passes, and 37 interceptions. Attendance dropped by more than 8,000 fans per game.

A trip home from a Monday night 41–10 loss at Pittsburgh put things in a different perspective. Because of a problem with landing gear after takeoff from Pittsburgh early Tuesday morning, the Rams' charter was forced to make a precautionary landing in Cleveland. No one on the plane, pilots included, knew whether the landing gear would work properly. "I think we're all happy we're alive," said Robinson. "When they say, 'We're jettisoning the fuel trying to land in Cleveland,' I think it gave a lot of people some sense of perspective in regard to their lives." The plane landed safely, but attempts to fix the mechanical breakdown were unsuccessful. After several hours the traveling party and equipment were transferred to another plane. They arrived at the Los Angeles airport at 9:45 A.M., more than five hours later than scheduled.

With one week left in the season, Robinson resigned. He made his announcement in a hastily called news conference after standing next to owner Georgia Frontiere in the annual team picture at Rams Park. "It's just time for me to move on," the coach said.

Ironically the Rams finished the season in Seattle, where Chuck Knox was on his way out as coach and, fewer than three weeks later, headed back to the Rams. Knox's departure from the Rams after the 1977 season was motivated by differences with owner Carroll Rosenbloom. The Rams owner wanted a more exciting brand of football. "It wasn't a bitter situation at all," said Knox. "It was just a meeting of the minds. I do remember one thing C.R. said: 'You might be coming back here someday.'"

Knox's first year back was promising. His first draft pick was king-size defensive lineman Sean Gilbert, who hopefully would anchor the middle of the line in the tradition of Merlin Olsen. Everett passed for 22 touchdowns and had positioned the Rams for a big victory at San Francisco, which would have given them a 3–2 record, but the result was a 27–24 loss after tight end Jim Price dropped two passes in the open field. Knox brought his first team in at 6–10, twice the number of victories as in 1991, but attendance dropped another 4,000 per game to an average of 47,810. Fans and media blamed owner Georgia Frontiere and team executive vice president John Shaw for the decline.

Everett had difficulty coming to terms with the pesky media, which, when not talking about the phantom sack in San Francisco, criticized the quarterback for his "happy feet" and for throwing off his back foot. The quarterback's relationship with Knox was uneasy. Jerome Bettis represented another outstanding first-round draft choice in 1993, rushing for almost 1,300 yards, but after a 2–2 start the Rams lost nine of their last twelve to finish 5–11.

During the pregame broadcast of an October 28 loss in San Francisco, NBC broadcaster Will McDonough broke a story in which he suggested that because of stadium problems the Rams and Los Angeles Raiders would move. "In a year and a half, Los Angeles, the nation's second largest market, could be without its two teams," said McDonough.

Rumors circulated in Orange County of a possible Rams departure. Many in the area were hopeful that Frontiere would sell and that perhaps the Walt Disney Company would buy. John Shaw, Frontiere's principal negotiator, was contacted by representatives from Baltimore, which had lost the Colts to Indianapolis in 1984; St. Louis, which had lost the Cardinals to Phoenix in 1988; and Memphis.

Free agency was resulting in huge contracts for players, and franchises were forced to look for other revenue streams. Anaheim Stadium, built in 1967 and remodeled in 1979, was no longer an attractive venue. The Rams were unsuccessful in selling luxury suites, even when they were winning. Orange County was composed of thirty-one different municipalities. Anaheim was the largest at 300,000 residents. Getting municipal support for construction of a new stadium would be impossible.

Another nettlesome reality was the scene on game days at Anaheim Stadium, where huge blocs of fans, many transplanted from other parts of the United States, cheered the visiting team. Shaw, under fire from the media and Rams partisans in Orange County, kept his counsel and began exploring other options.

On December 24, 1993, Georgia Frontiere sat down with T. J. Simers of the *Los Angeles Times*. It was her first extensive interview in many years. "It's something you have to consider," said Frontiere, when asked if the Rams were considering a move. "If you were offered something that was so good for you and your family and your business, you'd have to look at it . . . it's just a fact of life."

Baltimore, for example, was reported to have offered a stadium lease for $1.00 per game and to let the Rams keep all ticket, luxury suite, concession, and parking revenues. The Rams reportedly were paying the city of Anaheim as much as $400,000 a year in stadium rental. The city also received 7.5 percent of ticket sales, 20 percent from the sale of luxury suites, and percentages of parking and concessions.

On the playing field Jim Everett's run had ended. On March 18, 1994, Everett was traded to New Orleans for a seventh-round draft choice. He moved from suburban Orange County to Las Vegas and began to put the Rams behind him. Chris Miller, a free agent from Atlanta, was the Rams' new quarterback. The Rams drafted tackle Wayne Gandy in the first round and selected a spindly wide receiver named Isaac Bruce in the second round. Miller and Gandy wouldn't last, but Bruce became a Ram for the ages.

The Rams were 3–4 and hanging on in the playoff picture when they went to New Orleans. What followed was one of the most bizarre games in franchise history. The Saints, leading 37–24, punted to the Rams late in the fourth quarter. The ball went into the end zone untouched, and the teams began to send their offensive and defensive units onto the field. Television went to a commercial break. The last sight on the TV screen before the commercial break was the New Orleans punter looking back at something taking place behind him.

The ball that landed in the end zone still was in play. The Rams' Robert Bailey quietly picked up the ball while no one was looking and set off for the opposite end zone. Before the Saints realized what happened, Bailey was running untouched along the sideline to an NFL record 103-yard touchdown return. Rams special teams coach Wayne Sevier had reminded Bailey that a punted ball in the end zone was live until a whistle stopped play. Sevier also rushed to keep the Rams' offense on the sideline, which saved the Rams from a penalty for having too many players on the field.

Toby Wright set a Rams record earlier in the game with a 98-yard fumble return for a touchdown, breaking free as he straight-armed the Saints quarterback, who was . . . Jim Everett! The former Rams quarterback had the last laugh, however, leading New Orleans to a 37–31 New Orleans victory.

The Rams held off John Elway and Denver 27–21 the following week to improve to 4–5 and keep their playoff hopes alive. It was their last victory as the Los Angeles Rams. A seven-game losing streak ended Chuck Knox's tenure as the Rams coach. It was obvious the Rams were about to vacate Southern California, their home for forty-nine seasons. The Rams were moving to St. Louis, Frontiere's hometown. "I'm a little numb, quite frankly," Georgia told Simers. "The future looks so bright, but I'm also sad that things were not able to work out here. I didn't want to leave California."

St. Louis had a 66,000-seat downtown indoor stadium under construction and offered numerous inducements that would allow the Rams to cover a $30 million payout to settle their lease with Anaheim, plus numerous new revenue streams. Included in the agreement was an unprecedented guarantee that at least 85 percent of the stadium's luxury boxes and club-level seats would be sold for the next fifteen years. The guarantee "got us over the hump," said Rams President John Shaw. "I think it's as good an economic deal as there is in football today. It's a deal, as far as economics are concerned, that will far exceed the Anaheim or Southern California opportunity."

In July 1995 many Rams staffers, players, and coaches bid farewell to Southern California. They looked forward to the new life that awaited, perhaps none more so than Jack Snow, the outstanding wide receiver from 1965 to 1975 who had carved a career in broadcasting and was coming to St. Louis with the team. Snow left his home in Seal Beach at the crack of dawn in early July and, driving almost nonstop, twenty-eight hours and 1,900 miles later, pulled into the parking lot at Mathews-Dickey Boys' and Girls' Club in North St. Louis. Mathews-Dickey would be home for Rams football personnel and football administration for one year while a 168,000-square-foot practice and administrative facility was under construction in a suburb west of the Lambert Field Airport.

Snow was anxious to get started but also wistful. He grew up in Long Beach and played almost one hundred games in the Los Angeles Memorial Coliseum, first as an All-America end at Notre Dame, which came west every other year to play the University of Southern California, and then as a receiver for the Rams. Once, on a sideline play, Snow caught a pass and went out of bounds, knocking over actor Telly Savalas. "Oh, —! I just killed Kojak," Snow remembered telling his Rams teammates as they huddled for the next play.

Succeeding Knox as head coach was Rich Brooks, who had been an assistant with the Rams in 1971 and 1972 and head coach at Oregon for eighteen years, most recently winning the Pacific 10 Conference and going to the Rose Bowl on January 1, 1995.

St. Louis, without a team for eight years, immediately embraced the Rams, who were stunned when they got off buses to take the field for their first training camp practice at Parkway Central High School. The team received a standing ovation from the 3,000 spectators. The Rams played their first four home games in Busch Stadium as the Trans World Dome was being completed. Busch, jammed to accommodate more than 58,000 persons, offered a tremendous environment. Fans could almost touch the players, they were so close to the field.

Isaac Bruce blocked a punt early in the opening game at Green Bay, and then caught a touchdown pass on the next play as the Rams defeated the favored Packers 17–14. Bruce's passion for the game and his humble nature immediately made him the favorite Ram. He caught 119 passes in 1995 and was "adopted" by an elementary school that bore his last name.

A fast start hid some of the Rams' lingering personnel problems. After a 21–19 victory over Atlanta that gave them a 5–1 record, Toby Wright opined that the San Francisco 49ers, the Rams' next opponents, were "sweating bullets." The 49ers indeed perspired on a warm Indian summer day in Busch Stadium but not because of their hosts. San Francisco walked away with a 44–10 victory, their eleventh in a row over the Rams in a streak that would reach eighteen by 1999.

Brooks's team flattened out and finished with a 7–9 record but won the inaugural game at the TWA Dome 28–17 over the Carolina Panthers. Tackle Jackie Slater completed a twenty-season career with the Rams by starting the game. Brooks was fired after a 6–10 finish in 1996. After a search in which several candidates were interviewed and one, Kevin Gilbride, turned down an offer, Shaw and Frontiere surprisingly turned to Dick Vermeil.

Twice a Rams assistant coach and a builder of programs at UCLA and the Philadelphia Eagles, Vermeil had been a college football and NFL television analyst for fifteen years after retiring from coaching at the end of the 1982 season with the Eagles. Vermeil's early coaching departure had been because he was, to use his words, "burned out." However, he couldn't resist the opportunity to go back into the cauldron. On January 20, 1997, the Rams named Vermeil head coach and president of football operations.

Vermeil put together a veteran coaching staff and set about to change the culture at Rams Park, installing a suggestion box in the team's cafeteria and encouraging a one-for-all, all-for-one attitude among all employees. The coach also was popular with the media because of his forthright and often ribald responses. He soon became known to St. Louis's huge electronic and print media simply as "DV."

Vermeil's first big move was to trade the Rams' first-, third-, and fourth-round draft choices to the New York Jets for the Jets' first overall selection. With that pick Vermeil chose Ohio State's great left tackle Orlando Pace. Spending the first pick in the draft on an offensive lineman was unusual, but Pace gave Vermeil's program some badly needed cachet. Improvement on the field did not come as quickly. What followed were two tough years, 5–11 and 4–12.

Vermeil and his assistant coaches sometimes worked until 1:30 or 2:00 A.M Monday through Thursday (after arriving at the office by 7:00 A.M.), strategizing and reviewing videos. Practices were long and brutal. Vermeil also was known to call a 6:00 P.M. staff meeting on Friday, a day when coaches usually headed home early. Friends were concerned that Vermeil was headed for a repeat of his earlier retirement due to burnout.

Vermeil began to come under criticism in his second season. The Rams lost six of their last seven games and were tired, dispirited, and grumbling. They struggled under the quarterbacking of Tony Banks and Steve Bono, and Banks infuriated Vermeil with an incident that began in the parking lot of Miami's Pro Player Stadium. Banks was on the first bus that was to return the Rams to the Fort Lauderdale Airport for the trip home after a 14–0 loss to the Dolphins. Minutes before departure, Banks bolted from the bus and did not return to St. Louis with the team. Banks was tall, athletic, possessed a strong arm, and was highly intelligent, but his immaturity and erratic play were leading the Rams nowhere.

The season ended with a 38–19 loss to San Francisco. Although it was not apparent at the time, the Rams found a quarterback. Kurt Warner, who made the team as the third signal caller in training camp, played the fourth quarter, completing 4 of 11 passes for 39 yards.

A few players who lived on the West Coast stiffed the charter flight home to St. Louis and went to their homes in the Los Angeles area. Todd Lyght was one player who did not return to St. Louis after the game for the season-ending team meeting. What was the point of listening to Vermeil talk about the future of the franchise when Lyght and others felt there was none? "I'm upset that I've played for eight years in this league without an opportunity to win," said the first-round draft choice of 1991. "The team we've got now isn't going to get it done."

It was a critical time for Vermeil and his staff. They did not waste time addressing several issues. They signed St. Louis native Trent Green as their starting quarterback, after Green led the Washington Redskins to a 6–3 finish that followed seven straight losses to open the 1998 season. Joining Green from Washington was offensive coordinator Mike Martz, who had coached with the Rams from 1992 to 1996.

The Rams traded Banks to Baltimore, eliminating any distraction to Green's arrival. They began to feel better about themselves. Vermeil relaxed some rules. Workouts would be shorter, there would be one minicamp instead of two, and training camp would be streamlined. A while later the Rams traded second- and fifth-round draft choices to Indianapolis for running back Marshall Faulk. He had posted outstanding numbers in five seasons with the Colts, but as a combination runner and receiver in Martz's offense, Faulk would ensure himself a Hall of Fame career.

It all seemed to be coming together, but disaster struck in the third preseason game. Green sustained a season-ending knee injury when the Chargers' Marvin Harrison hit him from behind with what many considered an illegal hit, although no penalty was called. Vermeil, emotional and fiery, was moved to tears the next day at his weekly news conference. "We will rally behind Kurt Warner and play good football," the coach declared. Skepticism was the operative word. But what happened next was the stuff of fairy tales.

Warner threw 2 interceptions in the first game but passed for 3 touchdowns and 309 yards as the Rams stunned favored Baltimore 27–10. Ravens coaches were in shock on a gloomy, quiet trip home: "How could we lose to *these* guys?"

"We will kick Atlanta's ass . . . we will kick Atlanta's ass!" Vermeil announced at the Wednesday team meeting before the week 2 game against the defending NFC champion Falcons. Warner was warming to his task. He completed 17 of 25 passes for 275 yards and 3 touchdowns. His passer rating was a near-perfect 144.2. The Rams won 35–10.

Warner pitched a perfect game with a highest-possible 158.3 passer rating in the season's third game, the 38–10 rout of Cincinnati. He completed 17 of 21 passes for 310 yards and 3 touchdowns. *Sports Illustrated* featured Warner on the cover of its next issue with the headline, "Who Is This Guy?"

Warner could hand the ball to Faulk, one of the NFL's premier running backs, or he could throw the ball to Faulk, lined up as an essential wide receiver. Faulk's speed was bettered only by his shiftiness. He could not be covered by a linebacker. The other wide receivers, Isaac Bruce, Torry Holt, and Az-Zahir Hakim provided earth-shattering explosion as they complemented Faulk.

The Rams returned home to face the 49ers, whose eighteen consecutive wins had brought them even with the Rams at forty-eight wins apiece in the all-time regular season series dating to 1950. Warner passed for 5 touchdowns, 4 to Bruce, as the Rams turned on their longtime tormentors, winning 42–20.

Blowout wins over Atlanta and Cleveland followed. The Rams were 6–0 when they came to their first critical juncture. A corps of national media arrived in Nashville, where the Rams would play the 5–1 Tennessee Titans. The Rams fell behind

21–0 in the second quarter, but they had closed the gap to 24–21 and were attempting a field goal to send the game into overtime. The Rams center, Mike Gruttadauria, was blocked into kicker Jeff Wilkins, and Wilkins's hurried 39-yard attempt was wide.

The media left with a different view of Vermeil's team. Instead of hearing the refrain of "Same Old Rams," the media now saw the team in a different light. The Rams were no longer soft. They had faced adversity in a tough environment and come away with the respect of their opponents and critics.

A fluke loss to Detroit followed the Tennessee defeat, then the Rams put together a seven-game winning streak. With a 13–2 record heading into the final regular season game and home field advantage for the playoffs, Vermeil rested his regulars in a 38–31 loss to Philadelphia.

A 49–37 victory over Minnesota in the divisional playoffs carried the Rams into the NFC Championship Game against the Tampa Bay Buccaneers. In a strange, surreal game, the Buccaneers held a 6–5 lead late in the fourth quarter. The Rams had scored only on a field goal and safety. Tampa Bay had kicked two field goals.

Ricky Proehl, the team's fourth wide receiver, was the unlikely hero of the Rams' 11–6 victory, clutching Warner's 30-yard pass on third down and 4 yards to go with 4:44 remaining, sending the Rams into Super Bowl XXXIV with Tennessee.

Proehl was virtually invisible for the first five games of the season. Hakim's groin injury pressed Proehl into service, and he worked his way into the receiving rotation as a third-down specialist. "I've played ten years, and the best I've been is eight and eight," said Proehl. "Never seen the playoffs. This is what I've dreamed about for years."

Mike Jones's tackle of Tennessee's Kevin Dyson saved victory for the Rams in Super Bowl XXXIV.

Warner also would make the big pass in the Super Bowl. The Rams led 16–0 at halftime. "Look at them over there, they're celebrating . . . go out there and win it," Titans coach Jeff Fisher implored his team at the beginning of the third quarter. The Titans battled back, tying the score 16–16. With 1:54 remaining Warner backed up, sighted Bruce down the sideline, and heaved the ball just as he was hit by a Tennessee defender. Bruce floated under Warner's pass, adjusted to the ball in mid-route, hauled it in, and sped away to a 73-yard touchdown.

The Titans marched right back down the field and were on the 10 yard line with 6 seconds left. Quarterback Steve McNair passed to Kevin Dyson at the 5 yard line. Dyson lunged for the goal line, but Mike Jones, the first veteran free agent signed by Vermeil in 1997 and an inspirational player, came over from his outside linebacker position and stopped Dyson a yard short of a touchdown.

Warner was the Super Bowl most valuable player with 414 yards passing and 2 touchdowns. Bruce caught 6 passes for 162 yards. It was a remarkable victory, and the season represented one of the greatest turnarounds in NFL history.

The Rams always knew how to make history.

About the Author

Rick Smith spent eleven years as a publications representative for the Rams. He did PR at twenty-three Super Bowls and two Pro Bowls. He has also worked as a sportswriter for the *San Diego Tribune* and as a writer/editor for National Football League Properties, Inc.

THE INSIDER'S SOURCE

With more than 120 Midwest-related titles, we have the area covered. Whether you're looking for th path less traveled, a favorite place to eat, family-friendly fun, a breathtaking hike, or enchanting local attractions, our pages are filled with ideas to get you from one state to the next.

For a complete listing of all our titles, please visit our Web site at www.GlobePequot.com. The Globe Pequot Press is the largest publisher of local travel books in the United States and is a leading source for outdoor recreation guides.

FOR BOOKS TO THE MIDWEST